Pearl

You are Cleared to Land

Deanna Edens

Deanna Edens

Pearl: You are Cleared to Land

Text copyright © 2018 Deanna Edens

Acknowledgments

Cover Photo by Bessewisser99

My sincere appreciation goes to Mrs. Elizabeth O'Bryan Coffin, Mrs. Sandra O'Bryan Newell and Lewis L. Laska for sharing their rich family history with me.

Special thanks to David Robert Edens Jr., Cheryl Estrada, Nancy Holloway, Barbara L. Jones, Geneva Lacy, Sue Pilski, and Pam Tindell for providing editing advice, and to Lewis L. Laska for contributing stories.

ISBN-13: 978-1986277419

Some of the anecdotal illustrations in this book are true to life and are included with the permission of the persons involved. Additionally, all portrayals of people living or dead are dramatic renditions of actual historical events. Some names have been changed.

This book is a work of creative nonfiction.

OTHER BOOKS BY DEANNA EDENS

CONTENTS

"What do dreams know of boundaries?"

— *Amelia Earhart*

PREFACE

Have you ever heard of The Pearl of Alaska? How about The Hillbilly Eskimo? Do you know the name of the woman who received the Wright Brothers' Master Pilot Award at the age of ninety-seven? Well, her name is Pearl and this is a story about her and her family and friends. To be more precise many of these stories *are* hers—authentic memories written by an amazing woman.

When I received an email from Libby O'Bryan Coffin inquiring if I might be interested in writing the story of her family, I was more than intrigued. Libby and her sister, Sandy O'Bryan Newell, were born in the mountains of West Virginia and their mother was part of the John Bragg clan. These two educated, insightful women created a program called "Braggin' Rights" (after the Bragg family name, of course) to encourage students to learn and write about the history of their own families. They have collected, over many years, their mother's books of poetry, pages and pages of newspaper articles, stories about their family, and the writings of their Aunt Pearl Bragg Laska Chamberlain, a noted pioneer aviatrix and educator.

Pearl was the first woman to fly her own plane from the Lower 48 up the Alaska Highway to Alaska. She worked as a flight instructor, bush pilot, cryptographer for the Pentagon, flew in five Powder Puff Derbies, and was also a WASP trainee and famous "99er." Pearl was a member of the UFO's (United Flying Octogenarians), and the mayor of Fairbanks actually declared a "Pearl Laska Chamberlain Day." Pearl died in Nashville in 2012. She was one hundred three years old! Pretty impressive, eh?

Libby kindly sent me packages stuffed full of Pearl's unpublished stories, and poems written by Oma Bragg O'Bryan, who was Pearl's sister, and Libby and Sandy's mother. She mailed newspaper articles, one written by Pauline Bragg Roth, and book chapters documenting family history, including some of Pearl's flights of fame. Enclosed within the overstuffed envelopes were letters of correspondence and photographs detailing the life and times of the Bragg family.

When Libby emailed me a classic black-and-white photo of Pearl standing in front of an aircraft I was captivated. I studied the lovely woman for a long time. She and her co-pilot were sporting matching knee-length halter dresses that flared at their waists. Pearl's light chestnut hair was tucked-in just above her shoulders and the grin on her face revealed self-assurance and evident pride. My attention shifted to the aircraft they were posing in front of, noticing the markings on the plane:

"Miss Powder Puff 1960"
NM AIR GUARD

(Pearl Bragg and "Mickey" Michelon)

"Alexa," I addressed my hoity-toity Echo Dot, "who is Pearl Laska Chamberlain?"

My high-tech, voice-activated device informed me, "Pearl Laska Chamberlain learned to fly in a Kinner Fleet Biplane in 1933 and held a pilot's certificate until she was ninety-seven years old."

Libby sent pictures of Pearl as a young child, snapshots of her bundled up in a parka standing by her Cessna 150, numerous photos of Pearl receiving aviation awards, and images of her as an elderly woman who clearly had a zest for life that still sparkled in her eyes.

After talking with Libby and Sandy on the telephone, I agreed to meet with them to discuss the possibility of writing this series of tales to assure that this very special history will be preserved over time. The stories contained within this novel are the authentic memoirs of Pearl Bragg Laska Chamberlain, along with Oma Bragg O'Bryan's works of poetry and noteworthy entries written by Lewis L. Laska who is Pearl's son. I have taken the liberty to use narrative authority to weave these anecdotes together and to revise original short stories and handwritten notes, which had not previously been edited.

I have included photographs, a few which are almost one hundred years old, and I apologize for the lack of clarity in some of the portraits contained within this novel. However, even though the quality of certain photos have deteriorated somewhat, they do tell stories when mere words cannot begin to do justice to the characters you are about to meet or the places you are about to discover.

I am very excited to bring you this fabulous collection of "Braggin' Rights" stories that begin in the early 1900s on Chestnut Mountain in Summers County, West Virginia. Tales about bootleggin' and learning to fly in the Appalachians are followed by adventures to exotic places. Narratives about living in the polar region and escapades of an aviatrix are accompanied by heartfelt memories of real-life victories and the sorrows of a lifetime. So settle down into the cockpit, buckle your seatbelt and get ready for an astonishing and amazing flight.

PRESENT DAY

Standing on the east rim of the Bluestone River Gorge at Pipestem Resort State Park, I gazed from the plateau to the scenic Bluestone River some one thousand feet below. The spectacular view of the majestic landscape nearly took my breath away. Sunbeams flickered through the bountiful lime-green foliage that was sprinkled with hues of mauve and lavender blossoms, indicating springtime was arriving in West Virginia. I could see thousands of yellow, pink, and purple flowers peeking out from under the leaves flattened by winter snows, and over a period of the last few weeks the woods had become a fascinating kaleidoscope of colors and a paradise of gorgeous spring wildflowers. The mountaintop resonated with the sound of chirping birds and squirrels swooshing about nearby. I took in a deep breath of the cleansing country air, sauntered over to the directory located outside of the McKeever Lodge and scanned the events listed on the billboard.

"Braggin' Rights" Exhibition
Conference Room #3
10:00 a.m.

I stole a glance at my watch, made sure I had a pencil and notepad handy and made my way toward the room where I would finally meet Libby O'Bryan Coffin and Sandy O'Bryan Newell face-to-face and hear their presentation about the John Bragg clan from Chestnut Mountain. By this time, I had thoroughly read the writings Libby had mailed to me and scanned each of the old-timey photographs she had sent. I was very familiar with the Bragg clan but was eager to hear the tales they had to share about this amazing family—particularly those about their Aunt

Pearl, the famous aviatrix.

I found a seat in the second row and squeezed in beside a woman who reminded me of my Aunt Shirley who had passed on over to the sweet by and by two years ago.

"I'm so excited to be here, aren't you?" she asked.

"I am," I replied. "I've been reading about the Bragg family."

"You have? Well, I'll be. Do you know Libby and Sandy?"

"Yes," I smiled. "Kinda."

"I grew up with their mother on Chestnut Mountain and when I heard they were giving a Braggin' Rights presentation I decided to drive up here to Pipestem to hear their stories."

"I'm planning to write a book about their family, specifically their Aunt Pearl, and figured I could learn a few things," I explained.

"You're going to write a book about them? Well, I'll be." She nudged me. "Hopefully they'll share some juicy tales."

The presentation was nothing short of amazing. They had photographs that were large enough for everyone in the audience to see and told stories that had been passed down from generation to generation. The tales were about the good old days, bootleggin' in the mountains and what it was like to live in the days before we had televisions and telephones. They shared some of the adventures of their Aunt Pearl, their grandparents and their mother, Oma. When they had come to the end of the production everyone stood and applauded enthusiastically.

I glanced over at the lady beside me and noticed she was ardently cheering. Again she put me in mind of Aunt Shirley and I involuntarily flashed back to the first concert I attended as a teenager. My Aunt Shirley had taken me to see Elvis Presley at the Civic Center in Charleston, West Virginia, and it was the first time in my life I had seen interaction between a star and audience members. Elvis threw towels and flowers into the audience and fans returned the gesture by throwing underwear, hotel keys and teddy bears onto the stage.

I don't mean to boast, but my Aunt Shirley had the arm of a major league pitcher and when she whipped out a sexy pair of pink panties and hurled them toward the stage, they smacked Elvis right smack dab between his eyes. My young impressionable mind curiously speculated on when it was suitable to heave a pair of undies at a performer and this notion, unfortunately, occurs to me at the most inappropriate times. When the lady seated beside me picked up her purse and started rummaging around in it—I gasped.

"Surely not," I thought. Sometimes my imagination runs rampant. She plucked out a roll of mints and offered one to me. I let out a sigh of relief and accepted her generous offer, purposefully shaking the vision of Aunt Shirley catapulting her underpants at Elvis from my mind.

I stood at the end of a long line of folks waiting to talk to Libby and Sandy and finally was able to introduce myself. "Hello ladies, I'm Dee and I enjoyed your presentation very much."

"Thank you for coming," Libby said as she shook my hand.

"If you have time I'd love to take you both to lunch so we can talk more about the book and I have a few questions I'd like to ask."

"Sure," Sandy joined the conversation. "How about we go to the Dairy Queen in Hinton? They have the best fried bologna sandwiches."

"And navy bean soup," Libby added.

"Great. I'll meet you there in about an hour if that will work for you."

"Perfect," they chimed in unison.

So, this is when *Pearl: You are Cleared to Land* ultimately came to fruition.

"Bells on New Year's Eve announcing a new decade startled me. They were not only heralding the eighties but also tolling the end of my seventh decade. A few years ago when my son, Lewis, was a child he asked me what it was like in the olden days, olden days to him meant the turn of the century, and I, amused at the idea of having lived in the 'olden days,' promised to write it all down when I retired to the comforts of a rocking chair. He, now an attorney in Nashville, Tennessee, asks how many pages I have written. His prodding and my desire to tell what it was like to live without radio, telephone, television, electricity, automobiles, bathrooms and daily mail and at a time when children felt sorry for the man banished to the moon for burning a brush pile on Sunday, motivated me to begin my story..."

Pearl Bragg Laska Chamberlain

The Bragg Family
Back Row: Pauline, Irene, Grandma Cales, Laney Bragg holding Quincy,
Johnny Bragg, Pearl, Grandpa Cales
Front Row: Fred, Oma, Erma, and Coleman

INCIDENTS AT GRANDMA DORA'S

The first sign of the springtime bonanza coming to the mountains was when the chestnut trees showed a bright green hint of color. Pearl's fourth birthday had just passed and she had been invited to live with Grandpa and Grandma Cales for a spell. She had no idea why they asked her, the second of four sisters. She wasn't a particularly disagreeable child, and she didn't eat too much food... although she did occasionally fib when asked if she had scrubbed her teeth. *Why me?* She wondered, trying to recall precisely which incident had prompted this sudden exile. She couldn't imagine what it would be like to leave her home on Chestnut Mountain and live with her grandparents down the mountain in Sandstone.

Anyway, for some reason unbeknownst to her, it was decided, and her family piled into a wagon pulled by Morg and Bet and they bumped down the steep mountain trail. Her momma, Elaine, called Laney, held baby Oma on her lap while her poppa, Johnny, held the reins and kept his foot on the brake most of the time. Pearl and her sisters, Irene and Pauline, sat on a pile of straw in the wagon bed and held on for dear life, and since Grandpa's house was on a narrow ridge they closed their eyes to keep from seeing how deep it was down the cavernous ravine.

The first day at Grandpa Cales was pleasant enough. But the next day when Momma, Poppa and her three sisters left in the wagon Pearl had trouble holding back a flood of tears. That night when she had been tucked into her bed she buried her face in the pillow and cried herself to sleep.

After a few days she adjusted to her new home and in time she almost forgot she had once lived with her parents on Chestnut Mountain. Grandpa Cales' family consisted of Grandpa, Grandma Dora, Uncle Oscar and Uncle Eugene. Aunt Myrtle was married and lived on Chestnut Mountain. Uncle Fred, the restless one, left home at the age of seventeen and was railroading in Indiana. Uncle Oscar had scarlet fever when he was ten and never fully recovered, and Uncle Eugene tolerated Pearl so long as she was seen not too often and almost never heard.

Living with four adults and no children left Pearl with ample time to dwell in a world of make believe. She dreamed of kewpie dolls hiding under the silver maple and hoot owls that could talk. After all, Grandma Dora often answered her questions with, "A little bird told me." Middy blouses were popular and she dreamed of having one with a white skirt that would hold its pleats and never get dirty.

Days turned to months and most of the time she didn't feel needed in the home where idleness was the unpardonable sin. However, there were days when she felt quite helpful. Grandpa and Uncles Oscar and Eugene cut wheat with a cradle and hay with scythes, and on these hot harvest days she was kept busy taking water from the spring at the bottom of the hill to them where they worked in the field.

The house became a flurry of preparation for the annual visit of the threshing machine. The machine was used for separating wheat from chaff and straw and was pulled in by four horses and set up. An engine sputtered and belched black smoke but succeeded in threshing Grandpa's hundred bushels of wheat in one day providing it didn't break down.

Meanwhile, in the house Pearl, was kept busy carrying pails of water, peeling potatoes, stringing beans and helping pluck feathers from the chickens Grandma Dora had butchered for dinner. The threshers were neighbors who helped each other when the threshing machine came through, and there was rivalry between the women as to who could set the best table and have it ready at twelve sharp. Pearl figured her grandma must have been the champion, for she was efficient and a good cook too. She served fried chicken and gravy, green beans, boiled potatoes, applesauce, corn bread, piping hot biscuits, cake and pie. All was washed down with steaming hot coffee.

After the wheat and hay were harvested and the corn set aside, there was a pleasant lull before time to cut the corn, dig potatoes and sow winter wheat. Pearl's grandpa and uncles went to Sandstone, sat around the potbellied stove in Graham's store or on a bench on the porch, chatted idly, and argued about President Woodrow Wilson's policies or the Revenue Act of 1913. Grandma Dora took out her quilt pieces or mending laid aside during the busy summer days, and Pearl designed clothes for her corncob dolls. There was nothing exhilarating to do around the farm, but occasionally an invitation of sorts would come her way, causing young Pearl to feel like a baby calf in a field of clover.

You see, Grandma Dora was a member of the Ladies' Aid Society of the Sandstone Baptist Church and she was often invited to the homes of other members of the society for the noonday meal. Occasionally Pearl would be invited to tag along and she would always get gussied up and wear her Sunday dress. Pearl liked her pink checked gingham dress because it made a froufrou sound when she walked and her black button shoes were always shiny.

Pearl tried hard to please her grandma by being very quiet, and by following the general rule that children should be seen and not heard. She would always say, "yes, ma'am" or "no, ma'am" when one of the ladies addressed her and Pearl never started a conversation. She only spoke when she was spoken to.

Now, one should understand that Pearl's grandma was a conservationist long before Ralph Nader or Friends of the Earth came along. Nothing was wasted. Not ever.

When Grandma Dora butchered a plump rooster for breakfast, the feathers were later used to stuff a pillow and every scrap of meat was eaten. The feet were scalded to remove the scaly skin before she boiled the chicken, rolled the pieces in flour and fried it up in lard.

"The chicken's feet taste good, Pearl, would you like to try one?"

"Sure," Pearl consented.

Grandma Dora handed her one, and went about frying the chicken and baking biscuits. Pearl chomped on it a few times and concluded the chicken feet were pretty darn tasty.

Soon after, the Ladies' Aid Society met at the home of Mrs. Jack Richfield. The Richfield's ranked higher socially than Pearl's grandparents, and her grandma lectured her all the way there.

"You must be on your best behavior."

"Yes, ma'am. I'll try real hard."

"Promise?"

"I promise," she guaranteed.

Everyone sat down to a delicious looking fried chicken dinner and when it was Pearl's turn to be served, Mrs. Richfield asked, "Pearl, which piece would you like?"

"I'd like the foot," she answered.

The eyebrows of Mrs. Richfield were arched so high you could drive a team of horses through them. "Young lady, *we* don't cook the old scratchers."

That's odd, Pearl thought. "We do," she earnestly informed the group before redirecting her attention toward her grandma. "Don't we, Grandma?"

Grandma Dora let out a breath of hot air before offering a titter of a laugh. She then snuck Pearl one of those, "Wait until we get home!" looks. Pearl didn't completely understand what she had said wrong, but having spent a great deal of time staring at the woman seated across from her, she leaned in and asked her grandma, "What is that big lump on Mrs. Ruben's throat?"

"Hush," her grandma's lips fixed into the taut, pained shape they always assumed when she disapproved of her granddaughter's actions.

Mrs. Ruben's face turned a bright shade of crimson, while everyone else seated at the table dropped their gaze and curiously examined their fried chicken.

"What is it, Grandma?" Pearl insisted.

Grandma Dora articulately mouthed. "It's a goiter. Now, hush up!"

"Would turpentine make it go away?" the little girl whispered back, knowing full and well that three drops of turpentine on a lump of sugar cured most anything ailing ya.

Grandma Dora's face twisted into a shape Pearl had never seen before. "No. Stop asking questions!" she hissed through clenched teeth.

Pearl nodded knowingly and picked up her fork. She didn't murmur another word during the midday meal, but smiled brightly when the ladies glanced at her. She had a pleasant visit and the time passed quickly and she could hardly wait until the next luncheon. Unfortunately, she wasn't invited the following month.

"Not this time," Grandma Dora said as she styled her hair. "Maybe next month you can go with me."

"Why can't I go with ya this time?"

"Because I said so."

So that was the way the wind blew. Honestly, Pearl never really knew why she wasn't invited to attend a Ladies' Aid Society luncheon again, but figured it might have something to do with old scratchers. *Oh, well. They just don't know what they're missing out on.*

***

"Pearl," Grandma Dora pointed to the heap of clothes and dolls scattered across the floor, "you've made another mess."

"I'm sorry, Grandma."

"Why don't you grab the pail, run down to the spring and get some water?"

"Okay." Pearl dutifully walked to the back porch, picked up the water pail, trekked down to the spring and filled it three quarters of the way full. *I think I'll move my playhouse and dolls out to the barn shed so Grandma Dora will quit pestering me about chores.* She delivered the pail to the kitchen, snatched up her playthings and snuck out the front door.

The young girl found a quiet place in the corner, spread everything out so she could see it and pulled out the needle she had borrowed from her grandma. The scrap of fabric her aunt had given to her would make a perfect skirt for her doll so she threaded the needle and began sewing.

"What are ya doin' out here, Pearl?" she heard a loud voice shout from behind.

She turned to see her Uncle Eugene standing, with both hands staunchly propped on his hips—a sour look traversing his face.

"Nothin' much." Pearl shrugged her shoulders. "I was just making a skirt for Pinky."

"If ya drop that needle in the hay one of the horses could step on it and get it stuck in their hoof."

"I'll take it back to Grandma as soon as I finish up so Bonnie or Topsy won't step on it."

He pointed his finger and shook it furiously. "Return the needle now!"

Pearl knew better than to argue with an adult so she ambled back to the house and tucked the needle back into the sewing basket where she had found it.

"Pearl," she heard Grandma Dora call as the screen door creaked open, "let's go gather some poke greens."

Even though picking poke greens was the last thing in the whole wide world Pearl wanted to do, she tagged along and picked the leafy weeds with her grandma for over two hours. The entire time she kept thinking about how frilly the new skirt was going to look on her doll, Pinky, and was designing it in her head. *Maybe I can find a scrap of lace to sew on it. I wonder if a pocket would look good.*

By the time she and Grandma Dora made it back to the farm, Pearl was bubbling with excitement at the prospect of finishing the skirt she had started earlier. She sprinted toward the barn to fetch Pinky, Betsy, and the material she had left inside her makeshift dollhouse. Her grandma headed back to the house with a bushel full of greens.

When she approached the brow of the meadow, she saw her Uncle Eugene tending to a small bonfire in the barnyard. She stopped and stared for a long drawn-out moment. She could see Pinky was burning and he had just tossed Betsy on top of the blazing flame! She couldn't believe her eyes. She wanted to scream, and cover her eyes so she didn't have to watch Pinky and Betsy roasting in the fire.

Unfortunately, some things you can't un-see, no matter how hard you try. At this tender age, she understood that not only had she lost her beloved corncob dolls and all in the world that mattered to her, she also understood her Uncle Eugene didn't like her—actually, she figured, he downright hated her.

"Stop it!" she sobbed.

He turned to look at her, snickered and then turned his back to her.

Pearl was crushed. Her heart ached and the tears began to trickle down her cheeks. *How could he be so mean?* She crawled up into the hay above the trough and cried herself to sleep.

It was a very sad day in the life of Pearl Bragg.

***

Grandpa Cales' chest was kept behind a curtain in the corner of the upstairs bedroom. It wasn't locked but her grandparents told her to stay out of it.

"I don't want you meddling in things!" Grandma Dora warned.

The chest sides were metal with a curlicue design and wooden strips for reinforcement made it resemble a treasure chest. The lid was of the same design and rounded on the corners making it an uncomfortable seat on which things placed on its top would slide off immediately.

Pearl refrained from looking in the chest because her grandma was always around or took her with her when she went out. She also tried very hard to be the obedient little girl they wanted her to be and to fight against the ornery streak she felt well up inside her from time to time.

One day a nearby neighbor became ill. Grandma Dora got some mustard to make a poultice and Pearl pleaded with her to tag along.

"No, I'm afraid she might have typhoid fever. You stay here and keep out of things!"

Pearl knew Grandpa Cales and Uncle Eugene were hoeing corn in the barn field and wouldn't come in until supper was ready, so she tried to busy herself. She went to see the sitting hen then looked for sweet apples under the tree down by the cliff. She tried to play with Shep, the dog, but Old Shep just walked away. She wandered around the house and it wasn't long until she found herself upstairs, behind the curtain, staring at the forbidden chest. *Should I lift the lid?* She wondered. *One little peek won't hurt. What's in here that they don't want me to see?*

Inside there were several bundles of papers tied with strings. There was a yellowish colored dress, a ratty sort of veil, a book with dried roses that crumbled all over everything when she tried to pick them up. She found hand knitted baby socks with darned toes and heels, five locks of hair in envelopes, and an odd looking hat, which was too small for her head.

As she was about to close the lid, wondering why her grandparents were so fussy about such junk, she saw a paper rolled up and tied with a red and white ribbon. Pearl carefully untied it, unrolled the paper and there she saw a picture of a magnificent bay horse standing tall and stately. He was shiny, muscular and proud.

She attempted to roll the picture up when something went terribly wrong. It tore so easily causing a long horizontal slit across the bottom of the page. She gasped and her hand rose to cover her mouth. *Oh, no! This is horrible! The shame! Why did I look?* She gingerly closed the chest and prayed no one would see what she had done and in time it would go away.

No such fortune.

A few days later, Sam Cross came by with twelve dollars to repay her grandpa the money he owed him. Pearl started shaking in her shoes when she heard him say, "Dora, would you care to get Sam's IOU out of the chest?"

As Grandma Dora hurried up the stairs, Pearl took refuge in the clothes closet underneath the stairs, among the winter overcoats and boots. For hours she sat, hunkered down beneath the stuffy coats. *I wish a big old black snake would slither in here and bite me.* She tried holding her breath until she couldn't stand it anymore. *If they find me dead they'll be sorry.* She considered sneaking out and running down below the fence to where she and Pauline would play on the hanging grapevine and swing up as high as she could go. *If I let go at the exact right time I could break my neck and this will all be over. Then they'll really be sorry.*

Later she could smell supper and could hear them talking and eating at the table. She half wished they'd find her and give her a good beating, then she could feel sorry instead of guilty. The next morning she awoke in her bed. During breakfast her crime was not mentioned and just when she began to think all had been forgotten her Uncle Eugene came home from the store with a picture frame.

Pearl's grandpa asked, "What do you plan to do with that frame?"

"I'm going to frame Dan Patch's picture. You know there has never been as good of a horse as Dan Patch. I wish I could have seen him win a race." Uncle Eugene took down the picture of the Guardian Angel hanging above the mantel and replaced it with his cherished photograph of the award-winning racehorse.

From that day on, every time Pearl walked into her grandparent's living room her eyes would dart toward the mantel at the photograph of the elegant and stately, Dan Patch—whose poor legs had been half torn off. Pearl knew she should feel guilty. *But then again, Uncle Eugene did burn my dolls.* Her lips turned up in a half smile as she thought it all through.

***

"Would ya care for a slice of cheese?" Grandma Dora asked.

"Nah, I like candy better."

Pearl's grandma recognized that Pearl's family lived thirteen miles from town by the wagon road and seven miles down the steep bridle path. She also realized that while most of their food was raised on the farm, some things, such as coffee, salt, soda, baking powder and sugar had to be purchased at the store in town.

"Have you ever tasted cheese, Pearl? It's one of your mother's favorite treats."

"Yeah, I sure enough did. When Poppa takes the wagon to Mr. Deed's store he sometimes brings home a small bag of chocolate drops or peppermint sticks and Momma usually gives us her share because she says she likes cheese better than candy."

"Both are good," Grandma Dora said.

"I like candy better." Pearl walked over and dropped down in the seat at the kitchen table. "Did you know one time Poppa brought home a really big slice of cheese cut from a wheel on the counter of Mr. Deed's store?" She glanced at her grandma to see if she was still listening. "Irene had been pestering Poppa for weeks about bringin' us home some cheese and one day he sure enough did."

"Oh," Grandma Dora looked over the glasses perched on her nose. "Did you not care for it?"

"Well, I was expecting it to taste somethin' like candy and when it didn't I was kinda disappointed."

"I see."

"I quietly slipped away and hid my slice in a fold of one of the quilts Momma had stacked on a chair."

Grandma Dora arched her brow. "Is that so?"

"Yeah…" Pearl tilted her head. "I wonder if Momma ever found it. Anyway, Irene didn't sneak. Then when Poppa asked her if she liked the cheese she told him she was saving it for later.

This made Poppa mad, since she had been bugging him about it for weeks, then he took his pocket knife, cut a switch from the peach tree at the end of the porch and made her eat the cheese."

"Well, I can't really blame him. Times are tough and food can't be wasted."

"I know," Pearl agreed. "Irene ended up gagging, ran to the end of the porch and vomited."

"Oh. She didn't care much for it, I take it."

"I don't think she did." Pearl deliberated for a moment. "But I learned a valuable lesson."

"What lesson did you learn, Pearl?"

"I learned sometimes it's better to just sneak away and hide the evidence," the young girl confessed.

Grandma Dora's head dropped to the table. "Lord have mercy." After a long pause she added, "Sometimes I feel sorry for your momma and poppa."

"Yeah," Pearl dipped her chin. "Me, too. I don't know how they put up with Irene."

It was about this time that Grandpa Cales let himself in through the kitchen door. Noticing his wife's head was resting on the table he asked, "Are you all right, Dora?"

"I'm fine."

"Are you still sufferin' from headaches and all the ills of menopause?"

Her grandma lifted her head and pressed her hand against her forehead. "Yes, I suppose."

"How are you doin' today?" he directed his attention to Pearl.

"I don't feel very well either."

"What's wrong?" he asked, washing his hands with lye soap in the sink.

"Whatever's ailing Grandma is the same thing ailing me."

Pearl's grandpa started chuckling. Then he started coughing. He doubled over and smacked his knee. Finally, he sputtered, "Is that right?"

"Yeah," she nodded in assurance. "Grandma and I were just talkin' about what a stinker Irene is and it made both of our heads hurt and then our menopause commenced to flare up."

Grandma Dora and Grandpa Cales were eventually able to quit laughing.

"It's a good thing you have a guardian angel watching over you," Grandpa Cales said.

"I do?"

"Yep."

"Why?"

"Because you're so ornery sometimes, I think you're going to need an angel watching over you from time to time."

"Probably so…" Pearl willing admitted.

Grandma Dora giggled under her breath, rose from her chair and said, "Come help me with the ironing, Pearl."

"Yes, ma'am." She followed behind.

"Isabel is going to visit us for a few weeks, Pearl," Grandma Dora announced as she stoked the fire to heat up the wood burning stove.

"Who's Isabel?"

Grandma Dora tested the iron by running it over the edge of the linen shirt then placed it back on the stove.

"I don't think you've met her yet, but Isabel is the youngest child of the Richmond family and the only one who didn't marry."

"Why didn't she get married?" Pearl inquired.

"I guess she was just destined to remain single," her grandma said, pulling the scorching iron from the stovetop. "Could you place another iron on the stove for me, Pearl?"

"Yes, ma'am." She positioned the cold iron on the stove and watched Grandma Dora press hard against the fabric. "How old were you when you married Grandpa Cales?"

She seemed to ponder on this for a long moment. "Fourteen."

"Is that about the right age to wed?"

"I guess that'd depend on who you ask."

"Okay," Pearl replied, wondering who she could question concerning the right age for one to get married. "When's Isabel coming?"

"This afternoon."

"Why is she staying here?"

"Well, for years she was welcome in the homes of her sisters where she minded their youngins while they helped hoe corn and dig potatoes, but then the children grew up and she became just another mouth to feed, so she began staying with neighbors a week or two here and then on to another. She's going to come and rest for a while."

Pearl was surprised when Isabel arrived. Since her grandma had referred to Isabel as the youngest child, she wasn't expecting a sixty-year-old woman to be standing on the other side of the threshold when she opened the door.

"Pleased to meet ya, Isabel." The young girl shook the woman's birdlike hand.

"Likewise." Isabel smiled warmly.

Isabel looked much older than Grandma Dora, who Pearl thought was about forty years old, but she instantly fell in love with Isabel because she had a knack when it came to telling fascinating stories.

"One of my earliest memories," Isabel told Pearl, "was when a ragged, hungry bunch of Rebel soldiers showed up at our cabin and demanded food. My mama brought them plates of hominy with a side of fried meat and they greedily ate it all up before rounding up the pig, Bess the cow, Barney the horse, and all the chickens they could catch and left to join General Jeb Stuart in the Middle Ground. We didn't have much food to eat the following winter so we had to rely on wild game for our food that year."

Pearl's jaw dropped open in total disbelief. "They just stole all your stock?"

"Yep, they sure enough did." Isabel's nose crumpled up in revulsion.

"What else do ya remember about your younger days?"

"Let me think," Isabel raised her finger to her temple as if trying to conjure up a long lost memory. "My dear Daddy, now many years in his grave, went on horseback over a hundred miles to Charleston to buy salt. He always tried to go durin' the dry spells so the salt wouldn't get wet and oh, what trouble he had tryin' to keep them sacks dry as he forded streams and tried to outrun the rain. One time his horse died on him while he was making the trip and he had to walk all the way home carryin' the salt and tryin' to keep it dry."

"He traveled a hundred miles just for salt?" Pearl repeated. "That's a long way."

"Yep, it is."

Isabel told Pearl of a year when it was so cold the leaves didn't grow no bigger than a squirrel's ear, no crops grew, and the wild game left to seek food further south. "That year there was one day when it became pitch black right smack dab in the middle of the day. It was so dark the chickens went to roost."

"Oh my goodness sakes," Pearl's hand rose to cover her mouth. "That's mighty cold."

"Uh-hum," Isabel agreed.

"When we were youngins there was a grapevine down yonder and we would swing on it all the way across the stream," Isabel's eyes smiled when the memory suddenly returned. "Have ya ever swung on a grapevine?"

"Yeah," Pearl assured, "Pauline and I love swinging on the grapevine."

"It's a fine way to pass the day," Isabel replied, the woman's warm brown eyes misted over.

"It sure enough is," Pearl wholeheartedly agreed.

During Isabel's stay the young girl followed her around like a lost puppy dog. She enjoyed the fact that Isabel's smile was more the way her eyes crinkled up at the corners than the expression on her lips, and when it was time for her to move on to the Wheelers' house she didn't want to say goodbye. Pearl watched Isabel wash her face, comb her hair and tie on a blue bandana. She stared as the older woman put on the new gingham apron Pearl's grandma made for her and tied her wool stockings and faded apron into a red bandana. In the pocket of her skirt, Pearl noticed, she stored a handkerchief, a comb and an old pocketknife. Pearl wondered how she made out when her skirt had to be washed, but didn't dare ask.

Then with tears brimming in her eyes, she walked the mile with her new friend to the Wheelers' home. "You come and visit with us anytime," Pearl offered up before Isabel knocked on the door, "we'll always have a place for ya to rest."

"Thank ya, sweetie. I sure enough will."

After another week, it was time for her to walk up the mountain to the Jud Young home. The Wheeler girls, Elsie and Mamie, who were about Pearl's age, started walking along with her. When they were about half way there, they came to the place where the bend in the road wound around Sam Cales' Cemetery. At the bend, Isabel suddenly cried out, "Oh, my head!" and fell down hard on the ground.

Elsie and Mamie tenderly cushioned her head with leaves that had fallen from a nearby chestnut tree, and started asking her questions.

"How do ya feel?"

"What's wrong, Isabel?"

When she didn't respond to their questions, Elsie stayed with her while Mamie ran home for help.

"I'll be right back," Mamie promised.

Neighbors came and carried Isabel's body to the Wheelers' home where the women bathed her, combed her hair, put two pennies on her eyes to keep them closed, tied one of her bandanas around her head to keep her chin from sagging and dressed her in her blouse, skirt and new gingham apron.

In the meantime, the men looked in their barn sheds for lumber to make a rough box for a coffin. The coffin was covered with black sateen donated from Honaker's store and coffin handles came from Cantrell's store. Lining for the coffin was one of Grandma Dora's bed sheets that was bleached as white as snow.

The gentle rain stopped as they carried Isabel's coffin from the Wheelers' house to the wagon for the half-mile haul to Sam Cales' Cemetery. The neighbors who had readied her for burial, and other folks from up on the mountain, followed silently behind as the horses sloshed through the mud up the narrow road bordered by tall chestnut trees. Then hot tears streamed down Pearl's cheeks as she watched Isabel's body being lowered into her final resting place.

(Pearl at age 10)

GRAPEVINE
by
Oma Bragg O'Bryan

Oh, how free
in the forest green
I push and tug
on the grapevine swing
the limbs
are strong
some gnarled
some old
the grapevine swing
is something
to behold
around the hill
below the fence
we dash and swing
our heart's content

THE ONE-ROOM SCHOOLHOUSE

Standing ramrod straight and sporting his best Sunday-go-to-meeting shirt, black tie and black suspenders, Mr. Bragg respectably removed his hat before addressing the Board of Education, "I'm going to commence to sue this here school system if ya'll don't get a teacher for the youngins up on Chestnut Mountain fairly soon."

"But John," Supervisor Rhodes countered, "you know there's a shortage of teachers and we have been working diligently to find someone who is willing to move up here." He glanced around the table before adding, "We did manage to dismantle the school over at Rocky Bottom and rebuild it up on Chestnut Mountain."

The elected officials of the Summers County Board of Education nodded their heads in agreement.

"An empty schoolhouse is not going to help my children learn how to read, Charlie. It's almost November and school hasn't even started yet."

"We've been thinking on some ways to get a teacher up here," the supervisor assured.

"Well," Johnny Bragg rubbed his chin thoughtfully. "You can't plow a field by turnin' it over in your mind. I've contacted the Prosecuting Attorney's Office and I'm expectin' this mess will be taken care of shortly."

"Yes, it will, John. We received word today that a lady named Miss Grace, from over on Hump Mountain, has passed the state teachers' examination and received her number two teaching certificate. She has agreed to take on this assignment for the remainder of the school year."

Mr. Johnny Bragg dipped his head obligingly. "Alrighty then, so when will school start up?"

Supervisor Rhodes glanced around the room. "In two weeks," he murmured, "or shortly thereafter."

"Humph," Mr. Bragg snorted. "I reckon I'm going to have to take your word on it." He popped his hat back onto his head. "But if ya don't get this situation worked out in two weeks, I'll be back." He bowed his head politely and quietly exited the building.

***

When the news came that a teacher had been found and school would open on Monday, Pearl and her sisters were happy youngsters. She was living back with her family on Chestnut Mountain and the girls were out in the log barn making mud pies when the word arrived. They started hootin' and hollerin' around excitedly.

Pearl ran to the farmhouse. "Momma, Willard just stopped by and said school would be startin' on Monday. He said we'd need to bring our own pencils and paper."

Pearl's momma smiled brightly at the prospect, most likely imagining what it would be like to have the children out of the house for a few hours each day. "I've finished sewing your new dresses. All you girls need to do is polish up your shoes and rinse out your underclothes."

"Yes, ma'am."

"But first, go fetch some water and start it heating on the stove. Your poppa is bringing the galvanized tub in the kitchen for you to take your baths."

Is it Saturday already? Pearl wondered as she scurried out the door with an empty pail.

Pearl was scrubbing in the tub thinking about the two dresses she had to wear to school. Her favorite was a green poplin dress with a belt and buttons on the front, the other was a checked plaid, very plain dress except for the two patch-pockets her Aunt Myrtle had sewn on for her after she had tried and stitched them on crooked. Her momma, Laney, having made dresses for all four of the girls was tired of sewing and turned a deaf ear when Pearl had asked for pockets.

As she was drying off she decided her dresses would look better with lace edgings on the collars. She rushed upstairs and began crocheting and was almost finished when she went to bed on Saturday night. Since her momma insisted Sunday was the Lord's Day and did not permit unnecessary work, Pearl had to stay awake and wait until after midnight to add the finishing touches on the collar so she could wear it on the first day of school. Understandably, she wasn't going to take the risk of being banished to the moon because she had worked on a Sunday. So at precisely one minute after midnight, she carefully selected her needle.

***

When the ten-year-old girl entered the one-room schoolhouse, she consciously observed a huge wood burning stove in the middle of the room and rows of desks, each able to seat two or three students, facing the front of the small area. There were four boards painted black that served as a chalkboard and everyone hung their coats on nails in the back of the room and placed their shiny lard pails, which stored their lunches, underneath their coats as they arrived. A water dipper sat by the door and two of the older boys had been sent down to Richmond's spring at the bottom of the hill to fetch water for the bucket.

Miss Grace introduced herself to the class of thirty children and explained that they would have a visitor stopping by to inspect the building at some point during the day. "Be on your best behavior, children," she had sternly advised.

Later in the morning, Mr. Charlie Rhodes visited the one-room schoolhouse. He suggested there was enough scrap lumber lying around for the older boys to make a long recitation bench for the pupils to sit on when it was their turn to read. He glanced around at the expectant faces and pointed to Pearl. "Little girl, how old are you and what grade are you in?"

"My name is Pearl Bragg, sir. I'm ten years old and I'm in the first grade."

"Pearl," he scrunched his brow, "do you know if you had started attending school at the proper age you would be ready for high school in four years? Yes, in only four years."

Pearl pondered on this momentarily and suddenly recalled a passage her poppa had read to her many times.

> "When I was a beggarly boy,
> And lived in the cellar damp,
> I had not a friend or a toy,
> But I had Aladdin's Lamp."

Unexpectedly, the notion of getting through the eighth grade in four years became her Aladdin's Lamp. It was the very symbol of an impossible dream coming true and she was sure she could do it. Or at least this was the plan.

As the day progressed Pearl noticed Miss Grace, who was an attractive lady with long chestnut hair that hung in a long braid down her back, spent most of her time with the older students helping them with their work. She seemed to pay particular mind to the two oldest boys in the class, and when Pearl made the mistake of telling her she was ready to learn to read she was rewarded by having her face slapped—so much for a great start to the school year.

Humiliated, Pearl crossed her arms sullenly and gazed in silence through the window for a long spell and began wondering where the outhouse was. She had noticed the other boys and girls dashing outside from time to time but hadn't consciously processed where they were going to take care of their business. The need to know was now pressing.

"Ma'am?" she raised her hand high in the air. "Where do we answer nature's callin'?"

Miss Grace shuddered disgustedly. "Since the privies haven't been built just yet, I guess you'll need to *go behind* the towering chestnut tree out there." She pointed in the general direction. "The boys should be heading north down to the woods by the road," she added loud enough for everyone to hear.

"Thanks," Pearl replied apprehensively before sliding on her coat. Once outside, she discovered the ground was frozen solid and it took careful footwork to find a secluded spot to avoid stepping on the smelly mess made by others, and since the smaller children had heeded nature's call at the back of the building she suddenly understood what the common expression "thick as turds behind a country schoolhouse" meant—firsthand.

Fortunately for Pearl, Miss Grace didn't last long up on Chestnut Mountain. After less than a full year of teaching, she moved on and found a better job in the big city of Charleston and once again the students were left without a teacher.

Pearl and her sisters were free to follow their interests of playing in the woods and field when the weather allowed, and helping their momma and poppa with the chores around the farm—picking up loose rocks in the fields, bringing cows in from pasture, going on horseback to the grist mill on Saturday, and a dozen other little jobs, such as scrubbing the floor and washing the dishes. Luckily, the sugar maple trees had already been tapped, syrup made and stored in the fruit house.

On one particularly beautiful summer day, Irene and Pearl were out actively looking for something, other than chores, to occupy them for a few hours. Toys were unheard of, so Irene asked their poppa for his pocketknife to make a mulberry whistle.

"Be careful with it," he advised as he handed it over.

They found a few dead stalks on the other side of the fence and Irene soon had a fine-looking whistle formed. It was now Pearl's turn. Irene handed Pearl the knife and laughed at her clumsy way of trying to cut the stalks. Pearl was whittling away, literally destroying the best stalk. Irene kept laughing at her attempt to fashion the whistle, which started making Pearl as mad as a wet hen.

"Stop laughing at me," Pearl shouted.

The moment the words escaped her mouth the knife sliced deeply into her thumb causing waves of pain to radiate through her body. When the blood began spurting out, she started screaming like a banshee rooster. "I'm dying!"

"Hold it in the dirt until it stops bleeding!" Irene expertly informed her sister.

"Hold it in the dirt?" Pearl repeated doubtfully.

"Uh—yeah," Irene grabbed her sister's thumb and jabbed it deep in the red clay mud. "And don't tell Poppa because he won't let us use his knife again."

Pearl thought this all through and concluded Irene was probably right. Eventually her thumb sure enough did quit bleeding so she hid the cut from her momma and poppa and prayed they wouldn't notice. Suddenly she understood why folks advised to "rub some dirt on it" when an injury occurred. *"It's good advice,"* she prudently considered.

The morning after Pearl had almost lost a very important appendage, her momma arose from the breakfast table, looked out the window, just as the sun peeped through the maple and chestnut trees, and announced, "It looks like a good day so we may as well make soap."

Pearl knew a good day meant outdoor chores, which she enjoyed, with soap making being a major job. She also recognized her sore thumb might be a problem but vowed to suffer through. The cover was removed from the hickory ashes stashed away in an old tub. The tub was set on three large, flat stones, and a spout fixed under a hole in the bottom to let the lye drip into an earthenware crock. Pearl and her sister, Pauline, were given the task of carrying pails of water from a spring near the woods and pouring it on the ashes—not too much at one time.

As the water made its way through the ashes it came out tinted dark brown liquid lye. A huge iron pot had been placed on the sizeable stones and Oma, Pearl's younger sister, was in charge of picking up chips from the chip yard. During the winter, quite a bit of debris and chips had accumulated from cutting wood for the heater and cook stove and this debris was now being used and the yard was cleaned all at the same time.

Laney, in the smoke house, straightened and brought out all the fat saved from last season's butchering and excess from the table during the winter months. It weighed about fifteen pounds. She put the fat in the iron kettle and poured lye from the ashes, adding more as it dripped, until the liquid lye covered the fat. The fire was started and Pearl's sister, Irene, had the chore of stirring the lye-grease mixture.

The wind kept swirling around, causing Irene to walk around the pot in circles to avoid being overwhelmed by smoke. From time to time, their momma would check the mixture and add lye until all the grease disappeared. With the grease gone it was now only a matter of boiling the concoction down to the desired consistency. Pearl knew if soft soap was wanted it didn't take much more stirring, but Laney Bragg liked hard soap so she could cut it into cakes. She volunteered to help Irene out with the stirring. "Momma, I can take over for Irene if ya want me to."

Irene did not wait for her momma's answer. She enthusiastically handed over the ladle and Pearl began stirring. She put her back into it, trying to make each swirl effective. The wind switched again and the smoke soared into her face. She had been on stir detail for all of five minutes, but it seemed like ages. At last Laney was satisfied, dipped the mixture into the pans and cut it into cakes allowing it to harden.

Pearl let out a sigh of relief. When her momma glanced at the tub and said, "If you girls want to carry the rinse water over I think there is enough strength in the ashes to make lye for hominy," Pearl's heart sank. She was hoping her work was finished for the day and she would be able to take the horse for a ride.

"Okay," Pearl's shoulders sank. "Come and help me, Pauline. We'll run to the granary and fetch some plump, white ears of corn."

Pauline perched her hand on her hip. "Why don't you fetch the corn? I'll shell them, keep the plump kernels and save the nubbin end for the chickens."

Oma washed the kernels in warm water, then their momma put in the lye solution until the little black centers, called hearts, and the hard outer layers slid off. "It's time to start carrying water, girls."

Pearl, Pauline and Irene carried pail after pail until the snow white hominy was rinsed and rinsed until not a trace of lye remained. Their job was complete and they started singing:

"Hominy hot and hominy cold,
Hominy in the pot, nine days old.
Some like it hot, some like it cold,
We like it in the pot, nine days old."

"You're not quite done yet," Pearl's momma announced. "Pearl, I want you to run up to the Black's house and take them some soap and some maple syrup. Pauline and Irene, you get these pots cleaned up and put away."

"Oh, Momma," Pearl whined. She didn't want to do any more chores and her thumb was throbbing.

Her momma shot her a look and she knew it was in her best interest to keep her mouth shut and do what she was told. So she nudged Oma and informed her, "You're going with me."

Pearl's momma was a Christian woman and was always helping folks all over Chestnut Mountain and beyond with whatever they might be in need of, and Pearl knew the Black family was as poor as dirt.

"Why are we takin' this stuff up to the Black's house?" Oma asked as they trudged along the muddy path.

"'Cause Willard and his folks don't have much," Pearl explained.

"They don't have soap?" Oma probed. "Willard's patched overalls are always clean."

"I know, but they don't have much of nothin'," Pearl replied. "Just wait until ya see their house."

"What's wrong with their house?"

"It's a shack really." Pearl attempted to explain what she had overheard her poppa and momma talking about while they were rocking in the chairs and reading their Bibles on Sunday morning. "Ever since the mine closed down lots of folks moved into any old shack they could find. The Blacks found a two-room cabin over on Brooks Creek and since Willard's poppa lost his job in the mine, he tends to a garden and corn patch and hunts for meat for the family. I figure they eat quite a bit of rabbits, squirrels, possums, and ground hogs."

"What about Willard's momma?"

"I'm not sure he has a momma, but the woman who lives with them cleans houses for folks in town. I bet she walks over six miles to get to Mrs. Johnson's house."

"Every day?" Oma asked in disbelief.

"Yep, six miles there and six miles back home." Pearl stopped, turned and explained to her younger sister, "Willard's momma, or whoever she is, doesn't have a nose, so don't be surprised when ya see her."

Oma's eyes grew wide. "She doesn't have a nose? Where did it go?"

Pearl shrugged. "I don't know. Folks who live in coal camps settle their differences with whatever club or weapon they can find and she must have come out second best. I can only guess what happened, but it looks as if she has been clobbered with one of 'em homemade bats."

"I bet it hurt like the dickens."

"I would think so, too," Pearl admitted. "Don't stare at her nose. Okay, Oma?"

"I won't."

When the two girls rapped on the door of the old shack, a small woman with dark chestnut colored skin opened it. "Hello." She swiped her hand across her skirt tail.

"Good afternoon, ma'am. Momma told us to bring ya up some soap we made this afternoon and some maple syrup too." She handed the goodies over to the woman.

"Thank ya, you're very kind. Tell your momma I appreciate it."

"I will. Is Willard home?"

"No, he's out huntin' with his daddy."

"Oh," Pearl nodded. "Willard's my friend at school. He's a good boy."

The woman's eyes twinkled with delight at the compliment.

"Can I fetch you girls a glass of water?"

"Nah," Pearl glanced at Oma. "We better be gettin' back home."

Oma refused to look at the woman. She was afraid if she did look she might start gawking at the lady without a nose, so she glanced around the cabin and consciously took in the homemade table, nail keg chairs and a bed propped up on some boards. There were slits in the ceiling and walls that Oma could see through and she reckoned it probably got mighty cold during the winter and wet in the spring.

Pearl nudged Oma. "Okay, ma'am. Tell Willard we stopped in to visit and we'll see him when school starts back."

"Will do. Thank ya'll for stoppin' by."

Once they were outside and had walked several yards down the path, Oma turned and said, "They are poor. There's hardly any furniture in their house."

"I know. What'd I tell ya? Did ya see her nose?"

"No. You told me not to look at it."

"You didn't even glance at it?"

"No." Oma thought on this for a long spell. "But I'm going to make sure I'm kind to Willard when we're at school 'cause I feel sorry for him."

"Me too," Pearl glanced down at her aching thumb and decided it wasn't really too bad. "Some folks sure don't have it made like we do."

"That's for sure," Oma agreed.

***

In order to start the new school year, the Board of Education gave an emergency teaching certificate to a World War I veteran, Mr. Grover, who was suffering from the effects of Germany's poison gas. Not being a trained teacher he found teaching the thirty students a grueling task, and did not possess a particularly pleasant disposition.

Pearl had asked her poppa and momma if they could buy Willard a new pencil tablet and she felt good when she presented it to him on the first day back to school. He showed it to everyone and was as proud as a peacock. Pearl felt warm in her heart when she noticed Willard showing it off to the other boys. It had a picture of a cowboy on the front and the older boys seemed quite impressed. Even Mr. Grover commented on the five-cent pencil tablet, telling Willard he should take good care of it.

Mr. Grover quickly grew disinterested in teaching school and at noontime he took long walks alone so he could smoke and to be away from the students. By the time spring arrived his walks would last a little over two hours and the boys began to fist fight, call one another bad names—that Pearl would never repeat—and spit tobacco juice all over the floor.

"Mr. Grover?" Pearl asked, "Don't ya think it's dangerous to leave us alone while you're outside smoking?"

His eyes narrowed. He fiercely glared at the little girl. "What's your name again, kid?"

"Pearl," she reminded him. "Pearl Bragg."

"Well, Miss Pearl Bragg, if the time ever comes when I need your advice on how to run this school I will ask for it."

"Yes, sir."

His attention turned toward Willard Black. "Willard, did you complete your homework?"

"No, sir."

"Why?"

"It got wet."

"You allowed your pencil tablet to get wet?" Mr. Grover screamed, "Why didn't you put it in a dry place?"

With tears in his eyes, Willard sobbed, "Mr. Grover, there ain't no dry places in our house!"

"There ain't no dry places in your house?" the teacher repeated, with a hint of malice in his voice.

"Lots of folks have leaky roofs around here, Mr. Grover," Pearl interjected.

Mr. Grover glared at her. "Did I ask for your opinion Miss Pearl Bragg?"

"No, sir."

"Then shut up!"

Pearl realized why she didn't much care for Mr. Grover. He was downright as mean as a rattlesnake.

Just before bad became worse an epidemic of measles hit the school and the students were off for three weeks. When they returned they discovered Mr. Grover had resigned from teaching school, and had arranged a final oral reading examination to determine their placement for the following year. He suggested Pearl remain in the second grade, although he promoted everyone else, and her Aladdin's Lamp flickered and almost sputtered out.

On the long walk home from school Pearl intentionally lagged behind. She tore her report card into a dozen bits and shoved the pieces down a crayfish hole below the horse's watering trough. "Goodbye, Mr. Grover."

Once again Pearl and her sisters were free to help with the chores around the farm and greet the birds and flowers as they made their annual appearance. In between pulling the weeds in the garden, picking berries and canning them, peeling and drying the apples and churning butter, they gallivanted around in the woods, built a secret fortress, rode horses through the fields and chased fireflies at dusk.

As soon as summer arrived, it seemed it was already over.

Fall announced its onset with the changing of the leaves from green to ginger, yellow and crimson and it was time for school to begin once more on Chestnut Mountain. The new teacher, a blonde seventeen-year-old youth from Ohio, had graduated from high school and attended one summer term at Wilmington College. He wrote "Mr. Copeland" on one of the boards and said, "Address me as Mr. Copeland." From this minute on there was no question as to who was in charge.

Mr. Copeland had Ichabod Crane's philosophy of "spare the rod and spoil the child." His rod was a freshly cut hickory switch and he sure knew how to use it. His tactic immediately stopped all the bickering from the previous year that had gone on while Mr. Grover was out taking a walk and smoking, and everyone got down to the business of "the three R's."

"Children," he rapped a stick on the desk in front of him, "please show me your final report cards from last year."

Pearl could feel her heartbeat quicken. She glanced at Irene then studiously examined the blank sheet of paper on her desk.

"We didn't know we needed to bring our report cards back to ya," one of the children reported.

Pearl chimed in, "Mr. Grover didn't tell us we needed to bring our report cards with us."

Mr. Copeland sighed. "Okay. Just tell me what grade you are in when I call your name."

"Chester?"

"I'm in third grade."

"Irene?"

"Fourth grade, sir."

"Richard?"

"Fourth grade."

"Pearl?"

"I'm in the fourth grade." Pearl noticed Irene's eyes widened and she shot her sister a look that meant she'd whip the snot out of her if she opened her mouth. No one else said a word and Pearl was promoted from second grade to fourth grade in a split second. Her Aladdin's Lamp was shining again.

"Momma," Pearl and her sisters screeched as they cracked open the kitchen door, "we love our new school teacher!"

"Wonderful."

"Yeah, he's fun and he's going to teach us how to add, subtract, and multiply. He said so today."

"Very good," their momma replied distractedly. "Ya'll need to change out of your good dresses and get to your chores."

"Let's go, Oma." Pearl nudged her younger sister.

"Are ya going to tell Momma you're in the fourth grade this year?" Pauline asked.

"Nah, I'll surprise her with it later." Pearl turned and faced Oma, Pauline and Irene. "Ya'll better not tell her either!"

"I'm not sayin' nothin'," Oma said.

"Me either," Pauline agreed.

"Irene?" Pearl probed.

"I won't say anything."

"Good. I think I'm going to like school this year. Mr. Copeland seems like a mighty fine teacher."

"Whatever," Irene murmured.

Mr. Copeland allowed students to move along as rapidly as they could master a subject and made learning fun. In winter, when snow covered the ground the adjoining field was a maze of fox and geese trails, they played imaginative and spectacular games and were called upon to devise a plan to rescue their fellow team member from the prisoner's base, using the trails to guide them, and to exercise their best strategies.

On rainy days, with the desks pushed aside, they played lively games of Blind Man's Bluff. A fog of dust from the wooden floor brought coughs and sneezes as they rearranged the desks and went back to geography and history. Pearl soon mastered reading, writing and mathematics, even long division, and at the end of the year, much to her surprise, she was promoted to the fifth grade.

The following year brought a new teacher. Miss Barth, an eighteen year old from Ohio with a high school education was one of several who came from Ohio to ease the teacher shortage in West Virginia after the war. For the most part Pearl and her sister Irene were left alone to fend for themselves while Miss Barth attempted to make good students of the slow learners from the "ward bench."

Pearl soon understood Miss Barth did not have her predecessor, Mr. Copeland's, high opinion of the ability of these isolated mountain students. She was a lady with dreams and aspirations and this intrigued Pearl. *A woman who wants something more in life.*

Over Christmas vacation, Miss Barth asked Pearl and Irene if they'd like to visit the famous Greenbrier Hotel with her and the girls eagerly accepted the invitation. Pearl had never been in a fancy hotel and had heard many stories about the luxurious resort where the socially elite would rendezvous, so the young Miss Barth, with Irene and Pearl tagging along, walked down the steep mountain to the highway and hitched a ride some fifty miles to White Sulphur Springs.

In the lounge of the fabulous Greenbrier Hotel, Miss Barth wrote cards to friends giving the impression she was staying there, while Irene and Pearl watched the rich and famous walk around sporting their fine dresses and stylish hats. While Miss Barth was addressing the notecards, the girls sauntered around and peeked at the enormous dining room, the indoor swimming pool, and slipped into the grand Cameo Ballroom and pretended they were dancing with a prince. They couldn't afford a meal in any of the upscale restaurants at the resort, but Pearl had wrapped up some cornbread and dropped it into her handbag before they set out on their journey, so they nibbled on it from time to time when no one was looking.

"Come and look at this sign," Irene said.

Pearl walked over to where she was standing and read aloud, "The patrons of the Greenbrier are respectfully requested not to ask any employee to perform any service in violation of the prohibition law."

"Mr. Ward could make a fortune here, don't ya think? I bet he could sell his moonshine for double what he charges the folks on Chestnut Mountain."

Pearl started laughing out loud just thinking about Mr. Ward standing out by the entrance peddling his 'shine. "Or maybe we could peddle it for him?" she suggested goodheartedly.

Irene burst out laughing again and was still giggling when Miss Barth tapped her on the shoulder. "Are you girls ready to go home?"

"I guess," Irene said. "Thanks for asking us to join ya today."

"It's a ritzy place, isn't it?"

"It is," she agreed. "I'm glad I was able to see it."

When spring arrived, Miss Barth suggested Pearl take the final exam so she could graduate early. In order to do this she would need to board the C&O train #13 in Brooks for Meadow Creek where the eighth grade examination was proctored. The test was not terribly difficult, except for questions like, "What was the name of Rip Van Winkle's dog?" Her brow knit with concentration. She didn't know the answer since they didn't have any eighth grade readers at school. *Oh, well.*

Even so, Pearl managed to answer enough of the questions correctly and at the end of the day she graduated—two weeks after her fourteenth birthday. She later asked around and eventually found out that Rip Van Winkle's dog's name was "Wolf," and speculated on how this tidbit of information would be beneficial to her when she ventured out into this big, old world.

Ultimately, Miss Pearl Bragg was the first person on Chestnut Mountain to graduate from the eighth grade, and her Aladdin's Lamp glowed radiantly and would continue to blaze luminously for many, many years to come.

(The old schoolhouse, which later became a church, in a state of decay)

THE ONE-ROOM SCHOOL
by
Oma Bragg O'Bryan

The one-room school
Most a thing of the past,
There it stands all alone
Not long can it last.
With its desks all broken
The seats all gone,
The boards that were painted
Have now passed on.
The hooks on the wall
Where our coats once hung,
Are rusted and ruined
They can't last long.
The potbellied stove
The coal bucket, too,
Are no longer present
In the school I once knew.
The water bucket and the dipper
Then the water cooler, too,
Lead me to wonder
Where's the school I once knew?
The ivy is a climbing
Over the schoolhouse eaves,
With tendrils soft and tender
Hear the fluttering of the leaves.
The windows all around
With broken panes you see,
The bats fly in and out
Frantically dancing with glee.
The one-room school
Most a thing of the past,
There it stands all alone
How long can it last?

ON CHESTNUT MOUNTAIN

Maple bacon strips crackled and popped on the stove as Pearl impatiently drummed her fingers on the tabletop. "Oma, do ya want to walk down to the Waddell's with me after breakfast?"

"Sure. It's better than herding the cattle to the new ground."

"That's Irene's job," Pearl nudged her sister, "she's good at it. Now, let's go before Momma gives us more chores."

You see, once a week Pearl or one of her sisters would walk halfway down the mountain to the Waddell's home, because someone in the Waddell family would pick up the mail for the Bragg family at the Brooks Post Office and have it waiting for them when they stopped by. Fortunately, junk mail was unheard of, so their mail usually consisted of the weekly newspaper and sometimes a Sears catalog.

The paper had news items about several neighbors, sometimes who had ran afoul of the law by making and selling moonshine liquor. One in particular was Nathan Ward who was arrested for having moonshine in his possession, but Pearl knew Mr. Ward had mended his ways and became the pastor of the local church so he shouldn't be showing up in the headlines anymore.

Pearl would often pick some ripe cherries or wild strawberries and sneak off to the barn loft where she could peruse the pages to find out what it was like in the outside world and avoid being asked to run over to the gap to milk Old Pink, care for her younger brother or go fetch water from the stream.

The paper told of the Army recruiting young unmarried men between the ages of twenty-one and thirty-one who could read, write and speak English. She noticed the Democrats had nominated John W. Davis, who was from West Virginia, to run against President Coolidge in the 1924 election. An item of interest was of Pilot Lawrence Sperry's body found washed ashore near Rye Sussex. He had attempted to cross the English Channel in his flivver. It brought to her mind the three bombers that flew low over her one day when she was picking blueberries a few years earlier.

The advertisements posted on the back page encouraged readers to order slop jars for a little more than a dollar, or gingham fabric at twelve cents per yard. There was an entire page devoted to, "Why you should order your Ford now for two hundred fifty-five dollars straight from Detroit."

During this particular time, there was little cash on the farm from the weekly sale of butter and eggs—none of which trickled down to the children. Pearl's income for the summer was about three dollars. One of her cousins had paid her seventy-five cents to make her a dress, and she and her sisters searched for mayapples, blooming large white buds from underneath their umbrella-like leaves, washed and dried them in the shed roof and mailed them to Charleston. Since mayapples were selling for five cents a pound, they turned to selling ginseng, but unfortunately didn't have much luck. Pearl attempted to sell Cloverine Salve but gave up when she watched her neighbor, Mrs. Olson, having difficulty coming up with the twenty-five cents.

All summer long, day after day it was getting up early, work until eleven, go to the house and help cook the midday meal, which usually consisted of corn, potatoes, beans, fruit, occasionally pork and always a mess of cornbread. Pearl would then wash dishes and go back to work. Taking care of her younger siblings was part of her chores. She and her sisters also were in charge of weeding the garden, picking and canning strawberries and wild blackberries. The blackberries were somewhat difficult to find, but Pearl and usually Irene, would saddle up Old Bet and travel three miles to her poppa's old home place where, if they were lucky, they could pick eight or ten gallons before coming home, dog-tired, knowing the canning still needed to be done.

Even though Pearl worked hard, she knew she had it pretty good. Growing up in the hills of West Virginia, during the time when economic depression was on everyone's mind, she realized she was blessed to live on a farm. They had enough to eat and a roof over their head, which was more than could be said for some folks who were living on poorer, hilly patches of land.

They all knew their momma was expecting her ninth child and wasn't too excited. The small five-room cottage was already bulging at the seams. Little Erma, who was born with a cleft palate, required extra attention because at each meal she had to be secured in a highchair and cautiously spooned her food, and Pearl could only imagine what it would be like to have one more youngster to help tend to. Several times Pearl asked her momma if she could go to high school. Her answer was always the same, "There's no chance. You're needed here to help at home." But they both knew the reason was no money.

Time moved on with chores and more chores. It was a long summer with a whole lot of work and not too much fun. If the weather was favorable Monday was always washday. Pearl always hoped there would be kindling in the shed, because if not, she would need to find some broken limbs and brush in the woods nearby.

She or Irene would carry several pails of water from the spring and put it in a substantial iron pot underneath the apple tree in the chip yard. A fire was built and once the water was hot it was transferred to a tub of white clothes. Lye soap was added and then scrubbing on the washboard began. More water and lye soap were put in the kettle, along with the clothes and the fire stoked-up to boil the clothes. She used a broomstick to lift the clothes from the boiling water. They were then rinsed in cool water and another rinse to which bluing was added.

The last operation was starch, made from flour and water, and heated over the cook stove. Oma and Irene helped with the wringing, which all was done by hand, then the white clothes were ready for the clothesline. The colored clothes were then scrubbed and the very dirty clothes were boiled a little longer. By the time the last pair of overalls was drying on the clothesline the morning was gone and new chores began.

One night near the end of August, Aunt Myrtle came into the girl's bedroom. "Ya'll wake up and go get the boys, too. Your momma is having the baby so you're all gonna go with me."

"Where's Poppa?" Oma asked.

"He took the horse to Hinton to fetch Dr. Bishop."

"Why can't we just stay here?" Pearl moaned.

Aunt Myrtle raised a brow and sternly replied, "Because I told ya to come with me."

So that was the way the wind blew. All eight of the Bragg children walked up the path underneath the chestnut trees to Aunt Myrtle's house where they joined their four cousins, and they clambered into three beds and chattered the remaining hours away. After daylight Uncle Luther lit the fire on the cook stove and Pearl, Irene and Oma made the biscuits, peeled and fried apples and bacon and everyone settled in around the table to eat.

They washed up the dishes, and when they saw a tub full of clothes soaking on the porch, a jar of watermelon rinds ready to be preserved, and the garden full of weeds they intentionally resolved to ignore them all.

Cousin Amy suggested they slide down the straw stack, and the dozen of children, all ranging from three to seventeen, spent a few hours taking turns gliding down the stack like they were scooting in a sleigh down the steep mountain in a mound of freshly fallen snow. After lunch was over, and the dishes were washed up, they found quiet nooks and slept the afternoon away.

Sadly, when they arrived back home their poppa informed them, "Your momma had a difficult time giving birth to Hubert." Pearl wasn't sure exactly what this entailed but figured this was why Aunt Myrtle had come to fetch them in the middle of the night.

Hubert was a darling little fellow whose fingers began to turn blue. Then his skin paled and dark circles appeared around his eyes. Two days later, he was gone and Pearl felt terrible because she had resented his coming, thinking it was the reason why she couldn't go to high school. In a little casket covered with white muslin, she stood by and wept remorsefully as he was lowered into his grave underneath the maple on the hill.

She vowed to never mention "high school" again. Yet, sometimes things just turn out as they are supposed to, and one September morning when Johnny Bragg went to town to sell his butter and eggs he mentioned Pearl's desire to go to high school to one of his customers, Mrs. Lipscomb. It just so happened that Mrs. Lipscomb knew of the home of one Mrs. Rogers who wanted a girl to work for room and board in her home.

"Pearl," her poppa said when he got home, "I ran into Mrs. Lipscomb today and she said there is a woman in Hinton who is looking for a girl to work around her house in exchange for livin' there. It might be a way you can attend high school."

"Really? When can I start?"

"I don't know. Maybe you can take one of the horses to Hinton and talk with Mrs. Rogers."

"When?" Pearl bubbled with excitement. She was ready to mount Old Bet that very moment.

"Next week," he replied.

Pearl's heart sank. She knew when Johnny Bragg said something there was no need in quarrelling with him, and inside she was about as happy as a mule with a mouth full of bumblebees.

The following week, Pearl did make the trip to Hinton but was disheartened to discover Mrs. Rogers had already hired a girl for the job. She stared at the massive Summers County Courthouse with its octagonal turrets staunchly positioned at each corner. The grand Victorian-style structure towered over her as she passed by it on the street, making her feel small and trifling by comparison. Pearl's shoulders slumped. Her gaze lowered to the bluff, then even deeper into the valley where she saw just a peek of the New River flowing below, through the gilded leaves of autumn and the tears clouding her eyes. *There goes my only chance.*

Most fortunately for Pearl, the wind blew her toward her destination. Mrs. Lipscomb found out about the situation and suggested Pearl come stay with her until a suitable room could be found. "In fact," she said, "I have plenty of room so why don't you and Irene both come and stay with me?"

Pearl was giddy. *High school at last!*

On a bright, sunny day in October, Pearl and Irene scurried through the dried leaves down the mountain to the town of Brooks. She didn't care one iota that she only had one dress without patches. Near the Brooks Church they changed into their good shoes and stashed the old ones underneath a chestnut log. They rushed on down to the railroad track and flagged Passenger Train #14, paid the fare of sixteen cents each and rode to Hinton. The girls disembarked and walked ten blocks to the home of Mrs. Lipscomb.

School had already been in session for three weeks. On Monday morning they ate breakfast and set out in a downpour with Mrs. Lipscomb's daughter holding a gigantic black umbrella over them. When they arrived at school, they were directed to the office of Mr. Thompson and were assigned the classes of Sewing, English, Biology and Ancient History.

When noon hour came all the students went home for lunch except for Pearl and Irene who went to the bookstore to buy the textbooks and enough linen to make handkerchiefs in sewing class. Of their ten dollars, they only had enough for two pencils and one notebook.

The following day, Mr. Litchfield, her science teacher asked the class, "Can anyone tell me the definition of a mammal?"

No one knew, so Pearl held up a grubby hand—worn from hoeing corn, pitching hay and picking blackberries—and answered, "A mammal is born alive, has hair, breathes through lungs and suckles its young."

"You are correct! Nice job, Pearl," Mr. Litchfield praised.

Grace Pollack, a beautiful red-haired girl seated across from Pearl, gave the "for shame sign" but Pearl didn't pay her no mind. I mean, after all it was right there in the book.

In English class, Miss Cooper asked everyone for notebooks containing themes and other assignments. Since Pearl and Irene only had one notebook she asked, "Can we put our work together in the same book?"

Miss Cooper smiled. "No, I'm sorry. I will need to have your work separated."

Pearl could hear Grace Pollack snickering from the back of the room.

"Okay," Pearl replied, wondering how they were going to buy another book for their assignments. While they were walking home from the school that day the perfect solution occurred to her. Since bloomers were made of sateen, she found a scrap of the glossy material, a couple of discarded rings, and fashioned a homemade paste of flour and water and came up with her own notebook. The next day, Pearl handed her teacher the sateen covered notebook. Miss Cooper stared at it for a moment but didn't say anything, and then two days later, she handed out shiny new notebooks to the entire class. Pearl figured she must be fairly rich to be able to afford so many notebooks.

Eventually a light housekeeping room was found furnished with bare necessities. The toilet was downstairs and at the end of a wooden walkway. Pearl and Irene's poppa would sometimes ride the horse into town to give them some food for the week, or their momma would pack it in their bags on Sunday. Every Friday after school they would hike down the railroad track three miles and up the mountain another three miles. In November and December it was always dark by the time they reached home, carrying a bag full of heavy textbooks.

Laney Bragg was busy cleaning, scrubbing, mending, churning, and feeding chickens and fussed at them all weekend long. "Ya'll have your noses stuck in a book and I need ya to get up and help me tend to the chores!"

"Yes, ma'am." They knew they'd better get up and quit lollygagging around.

Every Sunday they hiked back down the mountain to board #14 to go back to Hinton. Since they only had a dollar each to get them through the week, and the train fare was sixteen cents each, they kept their fingers crossed hoping the train would reach Hinton before the conductor came through to collect the thirty-two cents. On these weeks they had more muffins.

While Pearl made good grades, she worried about being poor in the town where those from across the tracks did not go to high school. Her shabby dress in the prosperous town of Hinton was a blow to her self-esteem. The other girls in her class would pass her and Irene on the streets without even speaking to them.

"Doesn't it bother you when they don't say hello to us, Pearl?" Irene asked as they crossed Main Street.

Pearl nodded. "Yeah, it hurts my feelings."

"It just plum wears me out. They act that way because they have more money than us, don't they?"

"Probably," Pearl agreed. "Along with the fact that we're smarter than them."

Irene started laughing. "You might be smarter than them but I'm not so sure I am."

"You are," Pearl assured. "Do you know what, Irene?"

"What?"

"Whenever I start feeling bad because of how they treat us I just start thinking about Mandy and Harrison."

Irene stopped walking and turned to face her sister. "I don't recollect 'em. Who are Mandy and Harrison?"

"They live on the other side of Chestnut Mountain," Pearl answered, in a tone of voice, which indicated Irene should know who she was referencing.

"I have no idea who you're talkin' about," Irene barked back.

"Just let me tell ya the story about Mandy."

"Fine," Irene consented, and they continued to shuffle along.

***

The summer was cold and short. Leaves on oak and hickory trees grew no larger than a June bug and frost killed the corn tassels in midsummer. Harrison and Mandy were afraid—Mandy in particular. Without corn for bread, the chance of getting wild meat grew bleaker than ever and she wondered how they could feed their nine children when winter came. Yes, with a short potato crop and no beef or pork available there was cause for worry.

They heard about a meeting at the new Baptist church down on Laurel Creek and Mandy wanted to go. She knew she had no "fittin" clothes for goin' to a meeting, but a need for someone or something to rely on overcame her mended Lindsey skirt and Brogan shoes. Harrison had made Mandy's shoes and they did not fit very well. The left shoe was smaller than the right because he had ran out of cowhide when he was making them.

She and Harrison walked down the mountain trail, through weeds, thick grasses and red clay sludge. Long before the church was in sight Mandy was wet and muddy all the way up to her knees. From their place on the back pew they heard Brother Finch preach of a vengeful God, fire and damnation, God in his wrath, "Visiting iniquity of the fathers upon the children unto the third and fourth generation." He preached of the bad season as God's punishment for the wickedness of man. His theme was hell fire for everyone in the congregation unless they came forward and repented.

Harrison sat motionless when the invitation to come forward and confess was made. Mandy, seated beside him, wanted to go up the aisle and beg to be forgiven. As she was about to climb over his feet she glanced down at her bedraggled skirt and dirty Brogans. The closing hymn came and still she sat.

They didn't talk much as they climbed back up Chestnut Mountain, because Mandy was mulling over Brother Finch's sermon. She decided to make a bargain, a secret one with the Lord, if he would help them get through the winter she would try to be good and in the spring go up the aisle and confess her sins. She wished she had a Bible and could read better so she could understand what God wanted. She knew it was not possible because she didn't know anyone who could read, and on the few occasions where signatures were required Harrison made a mark.

The Lord must have looked favorably on her proposition. True, they had no bread, and no milk because the cow had gone dry and the five hens scratched for bugs and worms but laid no eggs. Mandy's bargain with her God was made in early September, a time when hard freezes were expected. This year, however, cold weather arrived weeks later allowing time for a good crop of rutabagas, turnips and several cabbages to mature. As the rutabagas and turnips grew, so did the grass and the tall grasses attracted rabbits, which provided meat for Mandy's stew pot hanging in the fireplace. With her newfound confidence from conversations with the Lord there was food on the table every day. A deer grazing on dead grass in the new ground became a Christmas feast and leftover meat lasted for several days.

Mandy recalled her mother telling of an Indian woman digging roots and using different plants, so she began experimenting and found chickweed, and an unknown but abundant weed out in the garden, which spiced up the flavor of her food. Sassafras root tea was good and even better, after the first of March the sap surfaced in the trees. Everyone in the family worked hard tapping sugar maple trees and boiling the sap down to syrup and sugar. Mandy soon learned that the rabbits attracted a fox population, so Harrison made enough money selling fox skins to pay for seed corn and much needed powder and lead.

In mid-May the warm weather finally arrived and a new crop of corn peeped through the ground. The cow, Gussie, had a calf, and two of the hens survived and eggs started showing up in the coop. Her children were thin, but as spry as crickets. It was time now. The time Mandy had promised the Lord. Again she trekked down the muddy mountain trail to Brother Finch's church. But this time, when the altar call was made, she climbed over Harrison's feet, because her patched skirt and muddy Brogans didn't bother her at all—not one little bit.

***

"I'm guessing the story you just told me was to help me understand how blessed we really are and we probably shouldn't care 'bout what other people think of us," Irene thoughtfully revealed once Pearl had finished her tale.

"Yeah," Pearl pensively added, "Mandy believed with all her heart just like I believe in us. We're going to accomplish something important one day, Irene. You just wait and see. The Bragg girls are going to accomplish so many great things that our names will be recorded in history."

Pearl could never have known that her prophecy would come true, but nonetheless it did. Years later, Pearl Bragg would become known as a courageous and noteworthy woman in the field of aviation and her name would be recorded in history due to her illustrious achievements.

(The Chestnut Mountain home in a state of decay)

MEMORIES OF CHESTNUT MOUNTAIN
by
Oma Bragg O'Bryan

Bows and arrows, stilts, ukulele and whistle,
Clay horses, thorns and purple thistle.

The time we spent on a grapevine swing,
Or picking wild plums as the school bell rings.

Digging mayapple to buy us a ring,
Or bright red maple still turning.

Taking a bath, it's sure to tell,
When the skin is white, you sure look swell.

Over to the gap to milk Old Pink,
Running to the chickens, when we hear a mink.

Carrying our bucket for lunch at school,
Walking in puddles is against the rule.

Picking a bucket of red ripe cherries,
Then over the hill to the wild strawberries.

We carry in the wood for the new cook stove,
Bring in the water from across the cove.

We shell up the corn for the mill you see,
And pick up the chestnuts from under the brown chestnut tree.

PRESENT DAY

After leaving Pipestem State Park to meet Libby and Sandy in Hinton, I hopped on Interstate 64, took the Sandstone exit and clung to the eastern rim of the New River Gorge for about ten miles following Route 20. The road is perhaps one of West Virginia's best-kept secrets. It has twists and turns, scenic views and bald eagles flying overhead.

I slowed my speed as I entered Hinton's Historic District and noticed the brick-lined streets and early 1900s storefronts. Some were brick, some clapboard, but all had been recently renovated so as to keep the nostalgia of the town's past while looking as neat as a pin. I kept a lookout for the most popular Dairy Queen on the planet. It is the original home of the Hinton Hot Dog, which I knew was toasted on both sides and served with creamy coleslaw, diced onions, a dab of mustard and a secret hot dog chili sauce. Today however, I was going to try a fried bologna sandwich with a side of navy bean soup—maybe.

I gawked at the menu posted on the wall for several long moments. There were too many choices. *What should I order?*

When Libby and Sandy arrived we placed our orders. An attractive woman, about my age, with frosted blonde hair that was perfectly coiled asked, "What can I get for ya, honey?"

"A fried bologna sandwich, a side of navy bean soup and a hot dog."

"Do ya want anything to drink?" she prompted.

"Of course, I'll take a sweet tea and a Blizzard."

"What flavor Blizzard do ya want?"

Again, I stared indecisively at the selections: Snickers, Banana Split, M&M, Turtle Pecan Cluster, Oreo, or Butterfinger. *Too many choices.* "I'll take an M&M Blizzard," I hesitantly blurted out.

"Good choice." She wrote down the order, ripped the paper off the pad and clipped it onto a round metal holder, then twirled it so the order was facing the guy who made the food in the back. "Is this a to-go order?"

"No."

She eyed me skeptically. "You wanna bologna sandwich, a bowl of bean soup and a hot dog all for yourself?"

I nodded.

"Okay," she replied, adding a doubtful arch of her brow. "Do ya want me to bring the Blizzard to ya later?"

"Yes, please. I'm buying them lunch too." I pointed behind me. I waited for Libby and Sandy to place their orders, paid the bill, and then we chitchatted for a few minutes while standing by the counter. I could smell the bologna frying and it triggered my mouth to water in anticipation.

"Dee, let's go into the dining room so we can see the view of the river," Sandy suggested.

"Sounds great to me."

I lugged my overflowing tray of food into the room with large windows overlooking the New River and we tucked ourselves in tight around the table.

"Do you think you'll be able to eat all of that food?" Sandy asked, tilting her head toward my tray.

"I'm going to try." I shrugged my shoulders before admitting, "I couldn't decide. Everything looked delicious."

"Anything you order here is scrumptious," Sandy assured. "You can't go wrong."

While we were gobbling down the delicious treats, I consciously observed Libby and Sandy. From a distance no one would have guessed they were sisters. Sandy was petite; her long dark hair was topped-off with a stylish hat, which made her look much younger than her age. Libby was a few inches taller, and sported a short blonde haircut and a free-flowing shirt. The main thing they had in common was their smile and their zest for life. I briefly wondered if they resembled their mother or their father—or perhaps a little of both. Libby's eyes were a striking shade of blue while Sandy's were dazzling hue of hazel.

Six years separated them and Sandy was just a teenager when Libby left home to attend college. As the years progressed they remained trusted and valued friends. The women where probably in their early to mid-sixties, but had more energy than people who were decades younger.

I glanced down at my half-eaten hot dog and full bowl of beans and realized I'd ordered too much food. *On the other hand I might manage to polish it off.* Pulling out my pencil and pad of paper I recapped the early tales of Pearl living at her grandparents, reviewed the stories of the one-room schoolhouse, and summarized Pearl's adventures while growing up on Chestnut Mountain.

"So, which stories do you think I should use next?" I asked.

Libby and Sandy glanced at one another. "Probably the anecdotes about Pearl learning to fly," they replied at the same time.

"Great. I'm ready."

LEARNING TO FLY

At the age of seventeen Pearl took a written test that gave her a "temporary" teaching certificate, thus blazing a trail of expectations for their younger siblings. Even though The Great Depression was affecting more and more folks at this time, she was able to secure a job as a schoolteacher and worked in one-room schoolhouses all over Summers County, including Tug Creek, Hurley, Rocky Bottom, Brooks and the Chestnut Mountain School where she had first started her education.

Then one fateful day, while she was visiting the Jackson's Mill 4-H Camp with her family, she met several pilots and had the opportunity to sit inside a plane. She traced her finger over the gauges in the cockpit and imagined what it would feel like to coast in the sky and look down on Chestnut Mountain from the perspective of the clouds. This momentous encounter would change Pearl's life forever.

Pearl had a secret dream as she trudged through West Virginia's snow and mud a mile and half down Chestnut Mountain, across Brooks Creek and another mile up Tug Creek Mountain to the one-room school where she was teaching. Her dream, come spring, was that she would have a few dollars tucked away to pay for flying lessons. Occasionally she would spy a plane high up in the sky and think, *Flying would be so much easier than hiking up and down these hills.* This was around the time of Charles Lindbergh and Amelia Earhart, and Pearl even had a brochure from a flying school in Lincoln, Nebraska, and hoped to go there. But the responsibility of helping two sisters in college made squirreling away a few dollars from her eighty-dollar a month check very difficult, and at the end of the seventh month of school the district ran out of funds and closed the schools.

What a blow! She had one hundred twenty-five dollars for flying lessons, but only thirty dollars for personal expenses. She found out she could learn to fly in Bluefield, which was only thirty miles away. So she got a room with kitchen privileges for five dollars a month and showed up at the airport with money in hand.

True, there were women already flying—Amelia Earhart and a few others. Unfortunately, there were none in or near Bluefield and she soon sensed what a dim view Harvey Amos, airport manager and instructor, had of women driving flying machines. Even so, Harvey accepted her one hundred twenty-five dollars so he could have his telephone and electricity reconnected, and went about bravely showing her how to use the stick and rudder in a Kinner Fleet Biplane.

She meandered about the sky "straight and level," and veered on takeoffs and bounced her landings. The Fleet was a ground looping fool but she conquered it with the help of Harvey's yelling and rudder kicking.

Some say ignorance is bliss. Hers was celestial as she floated on "cloud nine" anxiously waiting for each lesson. It didn't bother her to hike four miles to the airport to save the five-cent fare for a car. After all, a nickel would buy a loaf of bread, several cupcakes or a couple heads of cabbage.

After three weeks of lessons she felt good about her flying, despite Harvey's bellowing from the cockpit in front of her. Then one afternoon he found some excuse about having to be away the next day except for early in the morning and asked, "Can ya come in before seven o'clock tomorrow?"

"Of course," she beamed.

Pearl arrived at six o'clock and at dawn they shot a few landings. At around seven o'clock a road construction crew, on their way to a project south of the airport, drove up and parked. There were several trucks loaded with men, equipment and hefty cans of water. Harvey excused himself for a minute and went over to talk with them. Then he strolled back over and asked, "Pearl, do ya think ya can make it alone?"

Pearl nodded self-assuredly.

Harvey fastened his seatbelt across the seat to keep it from tangling in the controls, wished her luck, and she was off. The takeoff was smooth and straight down the runway, the flight was graceful and steady, and her three-point landing was perfect, providing no flames to douse.

A surprised and elated Harvey offered his congratulations. His plane was safe, but the road crew looked disappointed as they climbed in their trucks and headed for the worksite. The water cans were no longer needed to saturate the flames of a burning airplane, nor her midwinter dream of flight. Pearl crossed her arms in front of her chest and elatedly smiled those old water cans away as they bounced merrily in the back of the trucks inching down the dusty road.

"I'm gonna let ya start flying with Ernie," Harvey informed Pearl.

"Sure." She shrugged her shoulders. "Who's Ernie?"

***

Ernie learned to fly a Jenny in the late twenties and scraped up enough cash to buy an old Eagle Rock with a tired engine. On Saturdays and Sundays he hopped passengers off farmer's fields in the hills of Kentucky, Virginia and West Virginia. Some weekends he did well and made enough to pay his line boy, the farmer and have enough money left over for food and gasoline for the next weekend.

The Depression dealt him a low blow. People had to eat and it was a rare Sunday when he made ends meet. Ernie liked to fly, so when no one had any money he took a few hangers-on for free. All this came to an abrupt halt when Ernie was returning to his Webster Springs home field. He was above the jagged rock-strewn crest of Cheat Mountain when his tuckered out engine expired and Ernie was left with only one thing to do—land.

He picked out a spot between two spruce trees and hoped to have no greater damage than losing both wings. Unfortunately, the Eagle Rock's glide ratio did not allow him to reach the cliff he had chosen for landing and he crashed, breaking his vertebrae in three places. There was one thing in his favor though. An unemployed mine safety agent, who was gathering ramps nearby, came to the rescue and with his first aid "know how" was able to help. Ernie spent three months in the hospital and was almost as good as new, except for a dull ache that only disappeared when he had a stiff drink of moonshine every two or three hours.

Ernie was flight instructing for Harvey Amos and Pearl enjoyed taking lessons from him. When she first met him, all he had to say was, "Well, waddya know. A woman who wants to drive airplanes."

"Uh-hum." Pearl smiled coyly.

At the time, the flying business was slow but fledglings and more experienced pilots hung around the hangar and swapped horrendous stories of crashes and near collisions. At first, they refrained from hangar tales when Pearl was around because they figured these stories were not meant for a woman to hear. Later she was accepted and the yarns became as spicy as they were before she joined the group.

One bright, sunny Sunday in May, Pearl walked to the airport instead of paying the five-cent fare to ride in the streetcar. The weather was perfect, with the wind rolling down the runway, and she meant to make up the lesson she had missed on Thursday because of turbulence. You see, Ernie usually yelled, "Come let's roll out the Fleet and be off!" but on this particular day, he did not.

After an hour or so of hearsays and stories, Ernie turned to Pearl and asked, "Want to go to church with me?" He wiped his grease-stained hands on the sides of his pants.

Pearl glanced down at her long skirt and thick leggings, looked him straight in the eye and insisted, "I'm not dressed for church, Ernie." She made a swooping motion with her hand so he would notice her attire.

He smiled. "The holiness people where I go won't mind how you're dressed."

So off they went in Ernie's Essex Coupe.

As they zoomed along, he glanced over at Pearl seated in the passenger's seat. "'Tis only safe to make this trip on Sunday."

Pearl rolled her eyes and didn't ask any questions because by this time she knew Ernie quite well and was familiar with his devious means of outwitting the prohibition officers. They drove up East River Mountain to the Possum Ridge Turnaround. The road wasn't much wider than his Essex and the ruts were deep.

"What are we going to do if we meet another car?" Pearl queried.

"Don't ya worry 'bout it. We won't," Ernie guaranteed.

After three miles of furrows, rocks and bumps they came to a dilapidated shack with broken windows, boards missing on the porch and ragged children scurrying about.

Ernie explained, "This is Bob's house."

"Okay…"

Ernie called out to a young fellow who was peeping out from behind the pigpen. "Hey Cricket, this is Madam Queenie. Will ya take her down to the barn and show her your new pigs?"

Cricket came out and Pearl followed him down to the barn and watched the cute little Chester Whites with curly tails, all busy suckling the mother sow. Pearl thanked Cricket for taking the time to show her the piglets and slowly walked back toward the shack. She noticed Ernie give Bob some bills and then hopped back into the car to head down the hilly path of a road.

It was a steep road and if they dodged a tree on one side they could easily slam into a tree on the opposite side. Pearl held on for dear life as they bounced down the bumpy hillside. In an attempt to calm her nerves, she started jabbering. "Ernie, have you ever seen an addled duck?"

"Not that I can recall," he glanced over at her, before redirecting his sight on the narrow path. "Have you?"

"No, I haven't, but Poppa did. He had gone up on the mountain near Hix and came across some ducks that seemed a bit confused. He followed them through the meadow into the woods and finally to an abandoned moonshine still." Pearl hung on tight to the doorknob as Ernie made a quick turn. "Those ducks had been eating the corn from the sour mash and were drunk!"

Ernie started cackling. "Are ya kiddin' me?"

"No, that's the story Poppa told me."

"Well, waddya know." Ernie slowed his speed. "Did your poppa say exactly where the abandoned still was located?"

"No, Ernie." Pearl shook her head.

He grinned. "Just curious."

Her breath caught in her throat when he made a sharp right turn causing the back tire to bump in the deep ditch running alongside the path. Gunning the engine, he straightened the Essex Coupe and tapped on the brakes again.

"Ernie, my Uncle Lon has a still," Pearl blurted out.

"Is that right?" His interest piqued. "Is it on Chestnut Mountain?"

"I'm not sure exactly where it is, but Poppa and him argue about it all the time."

"Why?"

"Because Poppa works as a revenuer."

"Is that so?" Ernie glanced in the rearview mirror. "Does he work on Sundays?"

"I certainly hope not," Pearl grumbled.

She was more than relieved when the church came into view and they arrived just as the congregation was leaving. They blended right in with the Model T's as they proceeded to East River Road where they spied a revenuer's car parked and waiting at the Possum Ridge Turnaround. Pearl dipped her chin down low as they passed the revenuer's car hoping she wouldn't be noticed and they continued on, right smack dab in the line of churchgoers, until they could no longer see the official's vehicle.

Back at the airport, Ernie opened the trunk of his car, took a gulp from a half gallon fruit jar and said, "Come on Queenie, it's 'bout time we get to flyin', don't ya think?"

"It's about time," Pearl teased as they walked toward the hangar.

"Hey Pearl," Ernie said. "Have I ever told ya the Blue Flame story?"

"Not that I recall," she answered, sliding on a jacket overtop her white blouse.

Ernie exaggeratedly waved his hand in the air. "Neither faraway lands nor War Ridge across the river beckoned Arthur." He peeked at Pearl to see if she was listening.

A lopsided grin covered her face.

"Arthur was born on Chestnut Mountain and except for a brief stint in the Army during World War I, he never left. He had three interests in life, none of which included the fairer sex. Girls on the mountain came and went unnoticed. His dogs, Bruce and Dan, were at his side all the time and provided all the companionship he desired. Arthur's second interest was fox hunting, and his third liking was corn liquor."

"That's hard to believe." Pearl smiled wryly.

Ernie laughed. "Yep, I know. Anyway, between foxhunts he helped

Brother Lucas and Pappy Henry run off some of the best moonshine for miles around. Arthur was the self-appointed taster and many times he tasted until he became drunker than a skunk. Because of his tendency to drink too much, Pappy Henry limited his supply of 'shine and assigned him the job of sitting on a stump and watching for revenuers who just might happen by. Arthur didn't mind too much. He savored each sip from the small jar, rubbed Bruce behind the ears, and made mental notes of a better way to outwit the 'coon family that had been making raids on Pappy Henry's corn patch."

"Where's this story leading, Ernie?" Pearl asked as they made their way toward the plane.

"I gettin' to the point, Pearl, just hold on to your horses."

"Fine."

"Well, old Arthur was content with his lot in life and had no complaints as he dozed in the sun on that warm October day. Down in the valley a C&O freight train whistled. A hot box sent sparks flying into the tender, dry leaves along the track causing a fire that spread quickly. Smoke and flames billowed up the mountain, and all the nearby farmers and mountain dwellers rushed to protect their home by backfiring." Ernie paused for a moment. "Do ya know what I mean by backfiring, Pearl?"

"Yes, I do, Ernie." She motioned for him to continue.

"Pappy Henry, Arthur and Lucas hurried to their still to retrieve the precious copper worm and other equipment. They dumped the mash, put the barrels in the spring and carried the buckets and worm home. Meanwhile, Arthur went around the hill to a rotten hickory log to get three-gallon glass jugs of whiskey they had hidden there. The fire coming up the ridge seemed to pose no immediate danger and Arthur was weary from trying to outwit those pesky 'coons the last couple nights. He opened one of the jugs and took a swallow and then another. No one knew how much he had drunk before he fell asleep. Then as the fire roared up the ridge, Brother Lucas and a neighbor went to look for him. When they came in sight of the log, they saw blue flames rising from the broken jugs and arrived just in time to save Arthur."

"That is a cockamamie story, Ernie," Pearl said. "Let me recap. You are saying that Arthur was so drunk he didn't recognize he was in danger?"

"Yep," Ernie replied, adding a slight nod of his head.

Pearl climbed into the cockpit. "What's your point, Ernie?"

"My point is to never drink so much that ya fall asleep."

"Especially when you're flying," Pearl added.

He pointed his finger at her. "Exactly."

Pearl arched a brow in question. "This from the man who just guzzled down a pint's worth of moonshine?"

"Yep." He turned and gave her a sly wink. "Come on, Queenie! It's time we get at those stalls and spins. Ya ready?"

Pearl groaned. "I reckon."

(Pearl Bragg on the day she made her first solo flight)

From the Hinton Daily News

Hinton Around

"COUNTY TEACHER MAKES SOLO FLIGHT"

Miss Pearl Bragg, one of Summers County's first licensed aviatrix, and also a teacher, made a solo flight from Bluefield over the Hinton, Sandstone and Hix section on Sunday. Miss Bragg flew a Kinner Fleet Biplane. Miss Bragg has been receiving flying instructions in Bluefield for some time now.

BEYOND CHESTNUT MOUNTAIN

An almost empty pocketbook can be a challenge. It requires imagination and innovation to go places and have fun when there aren't any shekels to open travel doors. In May of 1934, school had closed for Pearl. For Addie, her friend and colleague, it had come to an abrupt halt in January when depleted funds meant the closing of several small schools in Summers County, West Virginia.

Pearl had been frugal all winter, helped to send a sister to the university and traded her Model A for a new Chevrolet. She could account for almost every dollar, as she deposited enough from her eighty-dollar per month checks to make June, July, August and September car payments and an extra twenty-five dollars for emergencies. She now had a whopping sum of fifty dollars in cash for the summer! Addie, however, was broke.

They formed a committee of two, held a lengthy ways and means session, ruled out going back to the farm and were on their way to Charleston to find employment. Hopefully! In Charleston they rented a room for five dollars a month. Addie found a job as a waitress right away at the Capital City Café. On the upside, she could get her meals for a dollar a day, but on the downside, tips were unheard of in this greasy spoon establishment.

Pearl continued to look for work. In the meantime she made out quite well on five-cent bread, peanut butter and overly ripe fruit and vegetables from a stand on the corner of Kanawha and Hale streets. A week went by. Pearl did not find work. Addie preferred Pearl's food to that of the Capital City Café when she saw the soup of the day being made from the scraps left on customer's plates.

The rented room was hot, and in these pre-DDT days, bed bugs added to their discomfort. At one o'clock in the morning, on an especially steamy, humid night neither of them could sleep. The streetlamp was shining brightly through the small window of their room and they could hear traffic sporadically passing on the street below. Pearl and Addie, stretched out on the lumpy beds, stared at the cracked plaster on the ceiling above them.

"I don't know which I like least, this hot room or my job at the café," Addie told Pearl.

"Did the boss pay you today? I mean yesterday, since it's after midnight."

"Yea, he tossed me a crumpled dollar as I went out the door."

"Then what's holding us? You have your payday and the car is parked out front. Let's really go somewhere, New York, for instance," Pearl suggested.

"Suits me!" Addie ardently consented.

In less than an hour, they were in the Chevrolet and on their way to New York City. They shopped for eleven-cent gasoline and were once fortunate enough to find some for nine-cents. The valves clunked and pinged as they moved along, seemingly congratulating one another for leaving Charleston and the Capital City Café far behind. They bought one five-cent Coke and shared it. Motels, little cottages with a bed and not much else could be had for a dollar per night. They worked out a schedule, drive one night and sleep the next. The problems were, unfortunately, that Addie couldn't drive very well and Pearl couldn't stay awake.

Nonetheless, they reached New York with over forty dollars and set out to see the sights—those that were free or nearly so. Pearl snatched up a discarded newspaper from a bench and scanned the advertisements.

"How does Guy Lombardo sound?"

"Great." Addie glanced down at her wrinkled skirt. "Where are we going to change clothes?"

Pearl scrutinized the area carefully and pointed her finger across the way. "Right there."

In the ladies' room of Central Park, they changed into their best dresses and shoes and made their way to the Waldorf Astoria ballroom where Guy Lombardo and his Royal Canadians were playing for ladies in flowing gowns accompanied by escorts sporting tuxedos. No one questioned them as they walked in and took a seat as inconspicuously as possible.

The next morning, in Central Park, they sat on a bench and shared a breakfast that consisted of a doughnut and a steaming cup of coffee.

"Do you know what Addie? This is really fun," Pearl said, curiously surveying the men and women scurrying off to work.

"Yes, it is."

"We've come so far on so little, why not see Canada?"

"I'm in," Addie concurred, popping her last bite of doughnut into her mouth.

In the Province of Quebec it was pouring rain. The roads were rutted and Pearl was sleepy. Sometime between midnight and daylight she veered too close to the edge of the road and slid into a ditch. She and Addie got out of the Chevrolet, examined the situation and instantly realized there was no way of getting out until help came. Pearl crawled into the back seat, slid her feet out the open window and fell sound asleep in no time.

When she awoke there was foggy daylight and several men standing around the car jabbering in French. One of the men looked at Addie, cowering in the front seat and asked, "Do you speak French?"

With her teeth chattering, she answered, "No."

The kind men pushed them out of the ditch and they made their way on to Quebec, went sightseeing down the narrow streets, had crackers smothered with peanut butter on the Plains of Abraham and counted their money. Their spirits were dampened to say the least. They decided to have a filling noon meal and skip dinner. It didn't work. By four o'clock they were digging in the back of the Chevrolet searching for whatever snack they could find.

"Have you found anything?"

"Just a rotten apple," Addie sighed.

"A rotten apple? How did we miss it earlier?"

"I don't have a clue." She held it out for Pearl to inspect.

Pearl's stomach churned. "Uh-hum. It's rotten to the core."

Addie tossed it over her shoulder.

"Hey Addie, what do you say we have dinner instead of getting a motel for the night?"

"Pearl," Addie pointed her finger at her friend, "that is the best suggestion I've heard all day."

They found a Mom and Pop diner and feasted on coffee and savory meat pies called "coffins." The crust was tall and straight-sided with sealed-on floors and lids and the meat mixed with mashed potatoes provided them with a satisfying meal. Afterwards they settled in the car for a long night's sleep. The next day they filled the gas tank and again counted their coins. Pearl had a dollar and fifty cents and Addie had a nickel. It was then that Pearl thought of John O'Bryan, the manager of Newberry Five and Dime store in Brattleboro.

"I have an idea, Addie."

"Is it a good one?"

"Maybe," Pearl divulged her plan. "Why don't we visit Brattleboro? I'll stop in and ask John O'Bryan if he will cash a check for me. I have twenty-five dollars for emergencies in the bank back home."

"We may as well try."

Pearl pushed down on the accelerator and off they went. They had no trouble finding the store and asked to see the manager. "May I speak to Mr. John O'Bryan, please?" Pearl asked, using her most uptown voice.

They could sense the envy on some of the clerks when the very handsome John O'Bryan greeted them warmly. "It's so great to see you again, Pearl." He gave her a light kiss on the cheek. "Can I treat you ladies to dinner?"

Pearl and Addie exchanged glances.

"We would love to go to dinner with you, John." Pearl graciously accepted his invitation.

He took them to a fancy restaurant, one of those places where you select your lobster from several swimming in a tank and the linen napkins are starched within an inch of their lives, and they gorged. The meal was expensive and Pearl calculated in her head, that the price of one dinner could feed both of them for two to three days—maybe four if they scrimped.

After dinner, John asked, "Do you need any help?"

"No," Pearl fibbed.

"Can I buy you some gas?"

"No, we are fine, John. Thank you for dinner. It was great to see you."

"Thanks for stopping by. I enjoyed our visit."

"Me too," Pearl gave him a sprite hug before climbing back into the driver's seat.

They headed south with their dollar and fifty-five cents and a gasoline tank, which was far from full. They stopped in Rhode Island, found a cheap motel and slept like queens until noon. Using Addie's last nickel they shared a cup of coffee, slipped into their best dresses and went to a bank in Providence where Pearl asked to see the manager to cash a personal check for ten dollars.

"I have been wrong on men, but have never made a bad guess about a woman," he smiled and handed her the crisp new ten spot.

"Are you ready to go home, Addie?" asked Pearl.

"I reckon."

The two friends hopped in the Chevrolet, rolled down the windows, and started singing, "I've Got the World on a String," as they headed down south to their homes on Chestnut Mountain.

***

It was a glorious autumn day in 1935, when Pearl and Oma meandered down to O'Bryan's grocery store in Hix, West Virginia, to pick up a few grocery items and to retrieve the mail. As Travis O'Bryan, who was filling in for the postmaster, was handing a letter to Pearl he reported, "Señorita Pearl, I have a letter addressed to you that came all the way from Mexico."

She practically snatched the sealed envelope from Travis's hand. She plopped down on a stool, took in a deep breath and ran her finger over the parchment before ripping off the end. "Hallelujah!" she waved the correspondence in the air.

"What is it?" Oma asked, sliding behind her older sister to peek over her shoulder.

"I have been invited to travel down to Mexico City to see how the school systems operate," Pearl proudly announced.

"When?" Oma queried.

Pearl carefully read the handwritten invitation. "Over Christmas break."

"Can I go with you?"

"Do you want to?" Pearl asked her sister.

"Are you kidding me? Of course, I want to go."

"Not that it's any of my business," Marion interjected, "but do ya think it's safe for two women to make a cross-country trip?"

"What do you mean?" Pearl posed, adding a tilt of her head.

"I mean, wouldn't it be in your best interest to have a man accompany ya?" He pursed his lips. "Just in case something happens along the way."

"Like who, Marion?"

Marion O'Bryan flipped his thumb over his shoulder. "Take Travis with ya."

"Take me where?" Travis walked from behind the counter to join in on the conversation.

"This letter," Pearl tapped it with her finger, "is an invitation to travel to Mexico over Christmas Break to see some of the schools and tour Mexico City."

"Mexico?" Travis repeated. "Sounds exotic."

Marion offered, "Can I buy you ladies a soda pop?"

"Sure," Oma replied. "Thanks."

"I'll pull out a map, too. So you can see how long it will take ya to drive there."

The four of them settled around a small table at the back of the store, sipped on their pops and carefully examined the map of the United States, Mexico and Canada that Marion had for sale in the store. "It looks to me as though you could drive through Chattanooga and then on to Birmingham," Marion suggested. "Of course, you'll need to get a currency exchange for pesos."

"Right!" Pearl made a mental note. They observed him as he traced the route with his finger. "You'd probably need to get a room there because I doubt you could make it much farther in one day."

"I agree," Pearl nodded. "Not to mention there are very few hotels available in the smaller towns."

"So true," Marion agreed. "Then ya could stop in New Orleans, which is on your way." He looked from one pair of excited eyes to the other. "I've heard New Orleans is one place everyone should see at least once in their lifetime."

"I would like to see a bayou," Oma admitted.

"Me too," Travis chimed in.

Pearl pointed to Mississippi. "Then onto the Magnolia State?"

Marion nodded. "I think so…"

Travis scooted his chair in closer to Oma so he could have a better look at the oversized map. "Then down the Texas trail to the border at Laredo?"

"Yeah, it looks like a good plan," Pearl admitted.

Just then they heard the cowbell attached to the front door clank to announce the arrival of a customer. Everyone looked up to see Carl Wilson bouncing through the door. "What looks like a good plan?"

"Oma, Travis and I are taking a trip to Mexico," Pearl told him.

"When?"

"Over Christmas break."

Carl kneeled down on one knee and begged, "Can I go with ya'll?"

Pearl glanced at Oma, who gave an ever so slight nod of her head, and then she glared at Carl prudently. A long pause proceeded her response, "Sure, why not? The more the merrier."

"Yee, haw!" Carl twanged with excitement akin to a toddler's. He got up, pulled a bottle of Coke from the icebox and scurried over to where the master plan was being devised.

"Here's what we are looking at," Pearl said, recapping their plan.

When the day finally arrived, Pearl and Oma packed their best skirts and store-bought blouses, along with their plain cotton dresses for traveling, and threw some snacks in their suitcases. Then the four friends took off for the trip of a lifetime.

When they stopped in Birmingham to get a room for the night Pearl pointedly explained to Travis and Carl, "All right, fellas, we have to stay within our budget here so we're going to have to share a room."

Carl let out a shrill whistle. "Ring-a-ding-ding!" he tooted joyfully and began dancing around.

Pearl and Oma rolled their eyes in unison. "Which means," Pearl continued with her elucidation, "that us girls will share a bed and you fellas will share a bed."

Carl immediately deflated.

"Additionally, we will be hanging a sheet between the two areas so we will have our privacy."

Oma added, "And there will be no peeping!"

"Of course not," Carl wiggled his brows mischievously.

When they settled in for the night and the lights were turned out, Pearl whispered to her sister, "I think Travis is smitten with you."

"Oh, he is not."

"Yeah, he is. He didn't even try to look around the sheet when we were changing clothes like Carl did. Travis is a keeper, Oma. He respects you, and he is an O'Bryan and all those boys are some good lookin' fellas. Heck, I've had a crush on Marion since I was knee-high to a grasshopper."

"Really? I didn't know you had a crush on him."

"Well, it's true. All I'm saying is don't dismiss the possibility."

"I won't. He is very handsome and kindhearted," Oma admitted. "But tomorrow night we're going to need to stretch the sheet tighter to keep Carl from ogling."

"Absolutely," Pearl agreed.

The trip down south went just as planned and they reached Mexico in record time.

"Alto," a man wearing a brown military-looking suit held up his hand.

"What did he say?" Carl asked.

"I think he said stop," Travis murmured, holding his foot firmly on the brake.

"Pesos?" the man demanded, holding up three fingers.

"He's saying we need three pesos to continue on," Pearl told the others. She leaned forward, stuck her head partially out the window and asked, "Do you speak English?"

"Si," the man said. "I do. Some. We must inspect your car and baggage."

"Okay," Travis consented, and they piled out of the Chevy.

Soon they were off again, admiring the towering cactuses, the dry plateaus and the mountains misty with moisture. The roads were narrow and unpaved and since it was the wet season in Mexico the rain and mud slowed them down. At one point, they were driving along taking in the new and exciting sights and a mudslide came rushing down the mountain. In no time sludge was gushing against the running board of the car.

"Oh, no!" Carl cried. "We're gonna die in a mud slide!"

"Hush up!" Pearl barked.

Terrified, they cautiously inched toward their destination.

Finally, they made it to Mexico City and were nothing less than astonished. The men were dressed in suits that were entirely white, which was a stark difference than to how the men dressed in West Virginia. They noticed people who had straps put together to form their shoes and observed the many chauffeured cars hurtling along at breakneck speed. They found the school and weren't really surprised that things weren't much different from the schools on Chestnut Mountain.

"Thank you very much for inviting us to Mexico, Mr. Lopez. This is my sister, Oma and our friends, Carl and Travis."

"I am pleased to meet you," Mr. Lopez offered a polite bow of his head. "Was your trip enjoyable?"

"Oh yes," Pearl replied. "We are excited to be here."

"I would like to take you on a tour of the city so you can see the shops and dine on some authentic Mexican cuisine."

"Thank you. We would enjoy it very much."

The kind and generous Mr. Lopez showed them around town. The crafts were vibrant and imaginative and the food was divine. They were able to visit the United States Embassy, on the Paseo de la Reforma, and the Floating Gardens with colorful boats (trajineras) drifting down the canal and bright flowers overflowing from the banks. The promenade was an unforgettable sight.

The days passed quickly and, in no time it seemed, they regretfully realized they had to go home. So they packed up the Chevy and headed back to Chestnut Mountain. All was fine and dandy until it was Carl's turn to drive. "It looks like the town of Thomas-and-Charley is coming up," he announced.

"Tamazunchale," Pearl corrected his pronunciation.

"Whatever," he pressed down hard on the gas and made a sharp turn.

A two-wheeled cart being pulled by oxen was stuck in the middle of the road. Carl slammed on the brakes, slid in the mud—to the left and then to the right—before his Chevy came to a stop, brushing ever so slightly against the brightly painted bullock cart.

Fortunately, they couldn't understand the derogatory slams that started rolling off the cart owners tongue.

Unfortunately, the local police showed up at that very second. He carefully listened to the cart owner's explanation concerning the series of unfortunate events. The officer frowned, and then his thick, dark brows creased together to form one large ridge that wrapped across his entire forehead. He malevolently stared at the reckless Americans before notifying them, "You are coming with me."

Carl started whimpering. "I can't be locked up in a Mexican big house for the rest of my life. What will Momma say? She'll be so disappointed. Oh, Lord. Daddy's gonna kill me. I'll never see daylight again."

Pearl, Oma, and Travis listened to Carl whine pathetically all the way to the station, occasionally soothing him with kind words.

"It will be okay," Oma assured.

"Don't worry, just tell the truth," Pearl advised.

"Shut up, Carl!" Travis barked.

They were escorted behind a wide, tall gate where they waited and waited. Then they waited some more. Eventually, a very important man, dressed in a light blue suit, came to speak to them. "Apparently your story of being school teachers visiting Mr. Lopez in Mexico City is true." He glared at Carl long and hard, creased his bushy brow in revulsion and spat his chew on the ground. "You're free to go." He pointed directly at Carl and said between gritted teeth, "Slow down. You are not in America anymore, son!"

Relieved, they hopped back in the Chevy and kept heading home, to the mountain state of West Virginia and their schools back at home.

(P.S. A little over a year later, Oma and Travis were married, and for their honeymoon they visited Niagara Falls and the Dionne Quintuplets in Canada. They decisively did not ask Pearl or Carl to accompany them on this escapade.)

(Pearl, Travis and Oma in Mexico – 1935)

From the Hinton Daily News

Hinton Around

"TEACHERS RETURN FROM TRIP TO MEXICO"

Pearl and Oma Bragg accompanied by Travis O'Bryan and Carl Wilson have returned from Mexico City where they spent the Christmas holidays. Miss Pearl Bragg said the trip was very enjoyable and everything went off without a hitch.

PRESENT DAY

Looking at my notes, something suddenly occurred to me. "I have a couple questions," I told Libby and Sandy. "How could Pearl teach before she graduated from high school? I realize that she took a written test, but…"

"Dee, it was common back in those days. She was very intelligent so she passed the required test and received a 'temporary' certificate."

"She was a good teacher too," Libby added. "Most of the Bragg girls ended up going into the teaching field. Aunt Pearl, Aunt Irene, Aunt Pauline and our mother, Oma, all taught school. The only one of the girls who didn't teach was Erma."

"Okay," I wrote it down and circled it twice. "I am guessing that the moonshining business was quite popular on Chestnut Mountain during the Prohibition."

Libby nodded. "Yes, it was. My Uncle Lon and Grandpa Bragg argued about it all the time from what I've been told. Since Uncle Lon was a bootlegger and Grandpa Bragg was a revenuer it caused quite a stir in the family. If I remember correctly, Pearl and my mother, Oma, even argued about it years after Prohibition was over."

"Yes, they did." Sandy interjected. "But, times were tough and people made money any way they could."

I tapped my pencil on the table in deep thought. "Yes, I suppose times were hard back then. I recall from Pearl's writings and from your presentation that Pearl had to scrimp and save to take flying lessons. Were your grandparents poor or fairly well off? The only reason I'm asking is because they owned a farm, which meant they had plenty to eat and a roof over their head."

"I've got this one," Sandy glanced at her sister. "Dee, it never ceased to amaze anyone how our grandparents, Johnny and Laney Bragg, accomplished so much with so little. They'd probably turn over in their graves if they learned about our run-away inflation and the amount of money we spend today to educate our children. They were education minded and wanted the best for their children. If I remember correctly, our grandparents often sold cattle to pay for their children to attend school."

Libby jiggled her head. "Yes, I do believe this is true."

Sandy held her finger up. "Hold on a second... I know Aunt Pauline wrote an entry for the *History of Summers County* and her final remark went something like this, 'As I reflect on our mountain top childhood experiences and the clean pure life that we lived, I feel that we are deeply indebted for our inheritance, to this wonderful pioneer couple who had true grit.'"

"Nice," I murmured. "Your grandparents must have been wonderful people."

"Mmm, hmm," Libby confirmed.

I perused my notebook and found a note I had circled earlier while listening to their presentation. "Okay," I cleared my throat, "in 1935, Pearl and Oma traveled to Mexico with Carl and Travis and they were not accompanied by a chaperone. Obviously, no one would think twice about it in today's times, but wasn't it a bit risqué back in those days?"

Libby smiled brightly and Sandy started giggling uncontrollably. "Dee, it was unheard of in 1935," Libby admitted, "but everyone knew what respectable young women Pearl and Oma were so people didn't assume anything. The community realized they were teachers and they were going on a business trip... so to speak."

"The newspaper article that was published indicated everything went off without a hitch." I wiggled my brow conspiratorially, awaiting their response.

"Well, if you're referring to the stopover at the Mexican jail, Mother indicated it was simply a slight hiccup."

"A slight hiccup," I repeated. "Carl certainly seemed concerned."

"Well, Daddy said Carl was the nervous type."

"I would have been somewhat nervous too," I admitted. "Okay...

and then your parents, Travis and Oma, were married soon afterwards."

"Yes, it was about a year later, and I believe they started falling in love during their trip to Mexico," Libby assumed.

Sandy started tittering again, and confirmed this assumption with a nod her head before briskly scooting her chair back and standing up. "I'm sorry. Every time I think about the trip to Mexico, I start laughing. I'll be right back. I'm going to run to the ladies' room."

I gazed out the large window of the Dairy Queen and took in the shimmering cerulean skies and the great blue-green, slow-flowing river. It appeared to be almost a mile wide and I briefly wondered if it had changed that much over the last decade. The New River was sparkling clean and void of pollution, and it was an amazing sight to behold.

When Sandy returned, I continued with my queries. "I think this brings us up to around 1940, when Pearl was still teaching and spending every moment she could find to fly. Where should I go from here?"

Libby and Sandy seemed to ponder on this for a long moment. "Probably, the tales about Aunt Pearl trying to get in enough flight time," Libby responded. Her attention turned to Sandy, "What do you think?"

"Definitely," Sandy agreed. "She had to have enough flight time logged before she could take the tests to earn her various certificates, or licenses, I believe they are sometimes called."

UP, UP AND AWAY

Pearl chose Davis and Elkins College in the summer of 1940 to renew her teaching certificate. During registration an announcement on the bulletin board caught her attention: CIVILIAN PILOT PROGRAM OPENS THIS SUMMER. One woman was permitted in the class of ten, and she hastened to take the military physical due to her age. At this time candidates had to be between the ages of nineteen and twenty-five years old and Pearl was now thirty-one. Fortunately, the midwife who attended her momma at birth had failed to record the event so she scribbled down her birthdate as being April 29, 1915, instead of 1909, and passed the physical without any problem. At summer's end with thirty-five hours of flying time, she passed the Civil Aeronautics Authority test and received Private Pilot Certificate #16889-40.

One of the ten who finished at Davis and Elkins was eligible for advanced training at Marshall College in Huntington. Two of the male students went into the Army Air Force, others either failed the physical or delayed getting their applications filed and again she was the only woman in her class, which consisted of twenty-five students.

They flew Waco UPF 7's, did the regular transition work and advanced to stalls, spins, loops, snap rolls, falling leaf, Immelman turns and slow rolls. The instructor, Mr. Howard, was invited to become Chief Aeronautics Inspector. He rode with his students and liked the way they flew. Having progressed thus far Pearl was assigned another course in preparation for an instructor rating. This course dealt with how to teach flying, except for the last five hours of Cross Country training. It was during this course that she and Mr. Howard flew into Charleston, West Virginia, and Pearl first saw Pi.

Pi was in a most unladylike position, upside down flat on her back, in the middle of the Kanawha River. Only her pontoons were above water and on them clung a wet flight instructor and his student who had been foolish enough to challenge a line squall. With gale force winds and rain mixed with snow there was no flying in Huntington. Mr. Howard invited her to go up river for a bowl of beans and corn bread at Irish Joe's. Over the beans they wondered about the stupidity of bucking a line squall.

"Do you think the aircraft will ever fly again?" Pearl asked.

Mr. Howard deliberated on this for long moment. "Well, I've seen worse. It will take some labor but I think it could be made air worthy again. I believe the rigging will be difficult to make like new, and flying it would probably remind one of driving an automobile with the frame bent in a wreck."

"It is salvageable, though. Right?"

He nodded. "Yes, I think so."

On their return from lunch they arrived just in time to see the red Aeronca Super Chief NC 31416 being pulled out of the river. Her fabric was torn, wings broken and propeller splintered. *Poor thing*, Pearl thought. She watched the water emptying from the interior as it was hoisted up the steep hillside.

In the months to follow Pearl worked hard to build up flying time and on one drizzling morning, when the sun rivaled with intermittent showers for control of the weather, Pearl plotted her course, checked the weather conditions and took off from Huntington, West Virginia, for Cincinnati, Ohio. She marveled at the panoramic view beneath her. She recognized the main road leading into town, its dark ribbon winding its way through the lush green countryside, then her attention turned to the wide sky ahead. The twenty-five students soon lost sight of each other and in due time twenty-four landed in Cincinnati.

As Pearl returned from the lunchroom she heard a radio message being relayed from Huntington, "We are requesting a search be instigated for the lost woman pilot."

"Excuse me," Pearl addressed the man seated behind desk, "I am the woman pilot and I have just finished eating lunch in the Pilot's Lounge."

"Oh?" A veil of a smile crossed his lips. "Uh… fellas, it's not the woman pilot who is lost," she heard him report with a note of steel in his voice.

The lost student found his way and landed safely an hour later.

Pearl added her flight time and was short almost a hundred hours of those needed before she could receive her commercial license and earn the rating of "Instructor." In early 1941, the Imperial Japanese Navy Air Service had not yet attacked the naval base in Pearl Harbor so when Pearl completed the third CPT course, she attempted to borrow money for flying lessons and was laughed at. Honestly, a few years earlier when Home Life Insurance Company learned that she was flying airplanes they had cancelled her policy. *Oh, well. They just don't know what they're missing out on.*

Feeling as though she was getting nowhere teaching, Pearl resigned and went to Washington D.C. where she worked as a waitress at the Marriott's Hot Shoppe. The pay was a little over eight dollars per week plus tips. Unfortunately, most of the customers were women government workers who were not known for their generous gratuities.

Still looking for a way to get the needed flying time she accepted a position with the Army Air Force as a cryptographer and was sent to West Palm Beach. The cryptographers, all women, were recruited to encode and decode secret messages and were on duty around the clock. Those not on shifts had extra time to spend the glory days of youth with the military men who were stationed nearby. It was during this time that Pearl received the very important message declaring, "Guadalcanal is secure for the Allied forces." Her heart was beating wildly and her palms were sweaty as she translated the critical dispatch. It was a moment she would never forget and she felt extraordinarily proud to be serving the United States of America.

Not surprisingly though, there was rivalry among the women cryptographers, and one very lovely girl showed up one Monday morning with a Chevrolet and a "C" gasoline ration card. Her fiancé had gone to boot camp. Everyone envied her as the rest of the women bummed rides to wherever they were going. They didn't head to the beach, mind you, because it was covered with blobs of oil washed up from ships that had been sunken by German submarines. The frothy, foamy waves had turned murky and dark so the coast was no longer an appealing place to bathe in the bright sunshine.

Later in the week, Pearl received a call from her CPT instructor, Mr. Howard. "Hi Pearl, how's it going?"

"It's going all right, I guess."

"Hey, I've decided to leave my job instructing for the military and I'm going overseas for a spell."

"Really? Well, good for you."

"Thanks," he paused, "I was wondering if you'd like to use my Taylorcraft while I'm gone?"

"Do I want to *use* your airplane while you're gone?" *That is certainly the understatement of the year.* "Seriously? Of course I do."

"Can you come and get her this week?"

"I'll be there by the time you hang up the phone!"

Mr. Howard chuckled. "Great. I'll see you soon."

Pearl took two days off and caught a bus to West Virginia. When she arrived she heard of the big news that had come to Chestnut Mountain.

"You're Poppa was featured in the *Agrico Crop News*," her momma proudly boasted.

"Really?"

"Yes, indeed. Everyone has been talking about it." She handed Pearl the newsletter.

Pearl began reading aloud:

100 BU MORE POTATOES PER ACRE WITH AGRICO
BETTER QUALITY TOO—SMOOTHER MORE UNIFORM,
EVEN-SIZED
By John W. Bragg, Hinton, W.Va.

"For thirty-five years, I have been using fertilizers… and always used to feel that fertilizers of the same analysis produced about the same results. But two years ago I switched to Agrico, and since then I have seen what a profitable difference Agrico makes. They were the finest-quality potatoes I ever raised—smooth, uniform and grading high."

"There's a picture of him in the newsletter, too. Poppa is a star!"

"Yes, he is."

Pearl celebrated Johnny's newfound fame with the family before returning to West Palm Beach with an airplane and an "X" gasoline ration card. The surprised looks of her co-cryptographers did not go unnoticed when she returned with such loot as an airplane with unlimited gasoline. In her mind, this compensated for all the days she went without lunch in order to fly once a week.

Pearl flew every chance she could get and even went in debt for more hours but was soon ready for her commercial flight test. Pearl's "cloud nine" sprang a leak when she arrived in Charleston. Since the Taylorcraft was in the shop for an annual inspection, she had to fly an Aeronca.

"I'm not going up in a plane that only has fifty horsepower," the inspector regretfully informed her.

"No problem," Pearl said. "I'll go rent a Piper Cub."

He pulled his pocket watch out and squinted at it for a long moment. "That'd be fine," he muttered. "If you hurry up." He added a grunt of annoyance, as she scurried off.

Now, since Pearl had never flown a Cub she was not familiar with its spin characteristics and spiraled down—swirling and twisting intermittently during the descent. She wasn't surprised when she failed the test and had to wait another thirty days.

Pearl was broke and now further in debt so she didn't waste any time. She continued to remind herself, "The quickest way to double your money is to fold it over and put it back in your pocket," and she saved and scraped and flew. In the Taylorcraft she practiced and practiced some more. She did so many spins she wouldn't have been surprised if it went into automatic spin when she throttled back.

Then on one of the smoggiest days she had ever seen, she flew to Connellsville, Pennsylvania to take the test again. The Civil Aeronautics Inspector looked at the soupy weather. "Let's start with some low work and maybe by the time we finish there will be enough visibility for higher work."

Pearl knew that low work consisted of flying a rectangular course, and figure eights on and around pylons to demonstrate one's aptitude regarding vital wind correction techniques. "Sure," she said, adding a smile that sparkled with self-confidence.

The low work went great and she nailed the emergency spot landing. So they progressed to the higher work that consisted of loops, snap rolls, and spins in which two turns were to be made with recovery not more than ten degrees from the heading at entry. All seemed to be going well until the inspector said, "Okay, let's go back to the airport."

While concentrating on the maneuvers, she had not thought about where they were. However, her guardian angel, the one Grandpa Cales had told her about long ago, must have had her hand on Pearl's shoulder that day, because when she turned to a one hundred twenty degree heading, and flew a few minutes longer, she spotted Connellsville in all its smoggy glory.

Back at the airport the inspector complained about his stiff legs, and took a long moment to rub his thighs before handing her a commercial pilot's certificate. "Good job, Pearl."

With a sigh of relief and a tear of joy in her eye, she whispered, "Thank you...I really appreciate this!"

"You've earned it," he verified.

Pearl practically swooned with gratitude.

A few days later she attempted the "Instructor" rating and since the United States was now at war she was successful and had no trouble finding a training job earning two dollars and fifty-cents per hour. She immediately contacted Glen Clark, owner of Kanawha Flying School. He had just received a Navy contract and was happy to give her a job at the new Navy War Training Service Sea Plane base in Charleston, West Virginia.

Mr. Clark asked Pearl to stick around for a pilot's meeting at dark, so naturally she agreed and met them at dusk just inside the hangar.

"I'd like to introduce our new flight instructor. Her name is Pearl Bragg."

The men nodded and murmured superficial greetings.

"We're having floats installed on the planes tomorrow afternoon and Pearl," he turned to face her, "you'll be assigned to NC 31416."

Pearl could see sneaky smirks forming on the lips of the other pilots in the room. She had completely forgotten about the red aircraft in the river until she saw NC 31416 in bold black letters on the wing. *Pi,* she thought.

Mr. Howard had been right when he predicted the planes rigging would never be the same and Pi was impossible to trim for hands off flying. At the end of the first day Pearl ached all over from physically compensating for the plane's poor rigging, so she started thinking about ways to motivate the in-house mechanics. It wasn't long until she hit on a scheme that worked.

Since it was wartime, everything was rationed—meat in particular. So she went home one weekend and discovered her father had butchered a fat steer. When she arrived back in Charleston, she gave the mechanics a few juicy steaks and they immediately became interested in Pi. On stormy days they would fix a little something here and another there, and when a new instructor was employed she was told he could have the plane—meaning she could upgrade to a newer one.

"If there's no objection," she smiled, "I would rather keep Pi."

"Are you crazy, Pearl?"

"Some would say so," she freely admitted.

Mr. Clark clucked with sympathy. "If you're sure."

"I am."

***

Pearl soon became intrigued by the Army Air Corp and thought if she became a WASP (Women Air Force Service Pilot) maybe she could continue to fly. She signed up and they sent her to Sweetwater, Texas, for flight training. She shared a room with six other girls and there was one bathroom for twelve others. The line in the morning was unbelievable, so she woke up before the chickens to race to the toilet.

When she first arrived, the bulky flying suits, called zootsuits, appeared to come in only one size—extra-large. Pearl, not having too much meat on her bones, could hardly move at times. With her chestnut hair curling at her shoulders, soft eyes, petite, feminine frame, she was the perfect picture of a wholesome southern girl. Not at all the type to be dressed in oversized combat-type overalls and heavy boots. But in spite of these little inconveniences, she worked hard, followed directions and didn't mind when she flew in an open cockpit through snowstorms, rain, extreme heat or sleet. She just wanted to soar.

Only weeks after her arrival in August of 1943, the British bombed a top-secret Nazi weapons base on Peenemunde Island in the Baltic Sea. Pearl read that the factory was producing new planes propelled by air rushing through their engines, and that some of the aircraft, called flying bombs, did not require pilots. Then on the 12th of September she learned of the Allies going ashore in Italy. News was reported of bombings and liberated territories over the next few months and she wondered how long World War II could continue.

It was on the very day President Roosevelt appointed General Dwight D. Eisenhower to lead the northern and western invasions of Europe, that she saw her name on the board, which meant that after only five short months they were washing her out. She was so mad she just walked out and decided to go to Alaska because she heard they desperately needed pilots and instructors. Pearl knew she was a good pilot, but also comprehended the program was winding down because the war should be ending soon and the men wanted their ferrying jobs back. *Oh, well. They just don't know what they're missing out on.*

She later found out they had orders to drop a certain number of women every day and felt as though she was just one of the unlucky ones.

***

When Pearl arrived in Seattle, she learned that since it was still war time everyone entering Alaska had to be interviewed before they were allowed to continue north. You see, Alaska did not become a state until 1959 and in early 1944 the Battle of the Aleutian Islands still affected the economy and citizens of the area. Americans were shocked that Japanese troops had taken over any United States soil, no matter how remote or barren and also feared that Japan's actions might be the first step toward an attack against mainland Alaska or even the Pacific Northwest. In short, this Japanese occupation was a blow to American morale.

Pearl patiently waited for over two hours in a large pale, yellow room with foldup chairs lining the sides of each wall. She was the only female in the room. Some men were slumbering with their heads tilted back against the wall, others occupied their time by talking to those seated near them, and some stared blankly into space while they waited. Pearl passed the time by reading *A Tree Grows in Brooklyn,* by Betty Smith that a fellow WASP had given her a few months earlier.

"Miss Pearl Bragg," the receptionist announced.

"Yes," Pearl stood up and tucked her book into her oversized handbag.

"Mr. Kincaid will see you now." The receptionist opened the door and provided a wave of her hand indicated she should enter.

"Please have a seat, Miss Bragg." The gentleman seated on the opposite side of the metal desk murmured without looking up.

She lowered herself into the chair, tucked her handbag in her lap and smiled confidently.

"May I see your application?"

She slid it across his desk.

He gave it a quick lookover. "So," his gaze rose to meet hers, "you think you want to go to Alaska."

"Yes, sir. I am sure."

"You do know it's colder than a well-diggers butt up there." His brow wrinkled in confusion.

"Yes, sir."

He stared at her intently. "What can you do?"

Pearl blinked. "What can I do?"

He exhaled deeply, shoved a cigarette into a black telescopic cigarette holder and lit it with a match. "What is your occupation?"

She struggled to keep her voice even, "I have a commercial pilot's certificate."

"A pilot's certificate?" His hand rose and he rubbed the crease in his forehead. "Anything else? I mean can you do anything useful?"

Useful? Seriously? Pearl wrung her hands nervously. "I am also a teacher."

He murmured something Pearl did not understand. "What else

have you done?"

"I worked as a waitress in the Marriott Hot Shoppe in Washington, D.C."

"Okay." With a resigned sigh, he stared at Pearl, placed his cigarette in the ashtray and scribbled his signature on an official paper. "Since you have experience as a waitress I'll add my stamp of approval." He plucked a date stamper from the desk door, compressed it with some force against an inkpad, tapped it on the document and slid it across the desk. "Here you go."

"Thank you, Mr. Kincaid."

"Good luck, young lady. You're going to need it."

***

That the thermometer was on the downside of zero was hardly noticed as Pearl made her way to the registrar's office for her first semester in college. Her ninety hours came from spring and summer terms and through correspondence and extension courses at the University of Alaska. For once she had enough dollars in the bank and a flying job when spring arrived. There was not a "cloud nine" on her horizon while the war raged on in both theatres. Pearl was so eager to complete her college degree that she registered for twenty semester hours, and among them were Alaskan History, Russian Language and Physics.

Waitress work had been a good stop gap twice before she came to Alaska, and it was essentially why Mr. Kincaid had given her permission to enter the territory. So, Pearl figured, "Why not again?" She agreed to wait tables in exchange for room and board because somewhere in the back of her mind lurked the ghost of the time when she had only one dress and not a penny. As Ben Franklin said, "A penny saved is a penny earned," and to save money would expedite her dream of aircraft ownership.

All was going well in her classes when someone in administration noticed she was a dyed-in-the-wool workaholic and sent a secretary to ask if she would be interested in cleaning house for Dr. Bunnell, President of the University of Alaska. She gratefully accepted the position and offers seemed to keep pouring in. On a cold Saturday in February the Territorial Road Commission Office telephoned.

"Hello?"

"Hello, is this Miss Pearl Bragg?"

"Yes, I'm Pearl."

"We were wondering if you would be able to fly Commissioner Woodrow Johansen from Phillips Field to Nenana," the man paused transitorily, "you would be using our aircraft, of course."

"Of course, sir. I would be happy to do so."

Pearl almost had a heart attack when she walked out to the Piper Cruiser with Commissioner Johansen and saw that the airplane was on skis. She had flown on wheels and seaplanes on floats but never had she flown on skis. As she paced around the airplane for a line check she tried to recall all she had read about skis. She vaguely recalled reading that skis were like flying without brakes. She certainly was familiar with flying without brakes, and had close to five hundred hours before she had the opportunity to fly a plane with brakes. She fastened her seatbelt with less confidence than she wanted him to suspect, squared her shoulders and took in a deep breath. Favorably, all went well and they landed in Nenana without incident. She flew the aircraft back to Phillips Field and made it in time to serve dinner to her tables in the dining hall.

Pearl remained busy throughout the semester. Sometimes she'd escape the humdrum of waiting tables and reading textbooks and walk across the campus, drinking in the cleansing air and towering spruce. She practiced Russian vocabulary as she went to sleep, between dirty platters and as she cleaned the president's house. After a Chinook, which is a period of good weather, Rainbow Skyways asked if she could come to Nome. They had the aircraft ready and students lined up.

"I am most interested but I will need to complete my final examinations," she explained.

"Of course. Thank you. We'll be looking forward to your arrival."

In early May, Pearl was halfway through her English Literature examination when all the bells and whistles at the university and at the nearby Ladd Field rang out loud and clear. It was Victory in Europe Day! Concentration was far from her mind, and how she passed the test she would never know. But now, with exams completed she was off to Nome via Wien Airlines, only to find the weather had a change of heart and the cold and icy weather reappeared like a bad penny.

Wien Airlines offered Pearl a bed in the pilot's dorm, which was a large room over top of the office. The local pilots had homes in town, and the dorm was used for itinerant pilots, those from Fairbanks and Anchorage who would stop and sleep overnight. There were two young Eskimo women who worked in the kitchen and had beds in the dorm, as well. Their beds were curtained off and they were required to obey a curfew. A Bureau of Indian Affairs spokeswoman told Pearl they were being kept isolated so they would be free of venereal disease come September when they would be sent to the Haskell Institute for further education.

Pearl had mixed feelings about this. On one hand, it was nice to know she was now accepted as one of the pilots, but on the other hand, as a female she didn't quite feel comfortable sleeping in the open dorm with up to four strange men. Nonetheless, when summer ended she had only praise for these pilots because they treated her with respect and the nearest thing she heard to a sexist remark was, "The S.O.B. weather means we're grounded in Nome."

Her living conditions meant eating out—a lot. She bought a meal ticket from the North Pole Bakery, which helped when the days were so stormy she didn't make enough to pay for her board. While the male pilots had a guaranteed minimum salary, she was on commission. In other words, if she didn't fly there was no money.

Pearl still dreamed of traveling and took every opportunity to catch a ride when she wasn't scheduled to fly, so when Wien had a charter to Saint Lawrence Island she tagged along. After landing, she didn't get to see much of the island, because she was required to sit on the tail of the DC3 to keep it from being blown over the bluff into the Bering Sea while everyone else leisurely went sightseeing. She regretted not bringing a headscarf with her to keep her wavy hair smoothed and away from her eyes, and by the time everyone returned to the plane she resembled a lion with an unruly and disorderly mane. She was startled when she caught a glimpse of herself in the reflection of the mirror—though no one else seemed to notice.

One interesting weekend she flew Safety Pilot for the local dentist to Candle to see his girlfriend. Much to Pearl's surprise, she was a WASP classmate of hers who had come to Candle to care for her nephews and niece whose mother had committed suicide. Years later, Pearl learned that her former classmate, Barbara Robbins, married Jon Lindbergh the son of the famous Charles Lindbergh.

On another interesting adventure, Pearl was sent to Moses Point to pick up a Wien mechanic who had been repairing one of their disabled aircraft. On the way back the engine sputtered and quit.

"Dive it! It will start," the mechanic yelled out.

"I don't think so." The adrenaline pumped through her veins. "I'm using these two thousand feet to find a suitable forced landing spot," Pearl persisted.

"Dive!" he screamed.

So she did.

The plane dropped like an elevator shimmying between floors and they landed almost immediately on the beach washing out the right landing gear.

Pearl was alive—or at least she thought she was—it was a little hard to tell. If she was dead, she figured, she wouldn't hurt like she'd been raked across hot coals. Her shoulders throbbed. Face, knees, hands... every single part of her body ached, including the thumb she had cut with her poppa's pocketknife when she was a child. She was out of sorts, totally discombobulated.

The mechanic started grumbling, "I scraped my arm and it's bleeding."

Through narrowed eyes, Pearl shot him an unsympathetic look. "Rub some dirt on it!"

It was eleven o'clock p.m. but still daylight in the Land of the Midnight Sun. There was nothing they could do but begin the long thirteen-mile hike up the beach to Nome. The walk was extremely painful for Pearl because she was wearing Eskimo soft slippers and her entire body was stiff. She vowed, "I will never again be foolish enough to fly without adequate footwear!"

As they were trudging along, the mechanic sheepishly suggested,

"Please don't tell anyone I suggested diving."

"I won't. It doesn't matter anyway, after all I was the captain of the ship and it was my responsibility."

"Once everyone learns of your landing you will become renown," he murmured, trudging along.

"Though it won't be desirable notoriety," Pearl pointedly reminded him.

She never claimed that it was the mechanic's suggestion to make the dive. She simply reported, "I goofed."

Only a few days after the above mentioned incident, the office called Pearl. "There's a woman in Wales who needs to be evacuated and you have the only plane in the field."

"Okay," Pearl agreed, wondering how she would fly and take care of an ill patient as she gassed up the airplane and filled out her flight plan. As she was preparing to take off another message came, "There is a Wien airplane that is closer and can be diverted by Wales for the patient. Remain at the airport to provide transportation."

Pearl waited and waited. Then as the Gullwing landed, she rushed out and opened the door as the pilot shut off the engine. He stepped out of the cockpit, motioned for Pearl to stand aside and vomited. The Eskimo woman had died during the flight. Knowing that when death occurs the muscles controlling fecal and urine waste relax, she guessed this is what had happened in this case. It was the odor in the closed cockpit that had made the pilot ill, and possibly the feeling of helplessness he felt for not being able to help the woman as he piloted the plane.

"Can you remain with the plane and the corpse while I go to town to arouse the undertaker?" he asked, swiping his mouth with his shirtsleeve.

"I'll stay here until you get back," Pearl promised.

Hours passed. Evidently, the undertaker didn't respond to the pounding on his door, so Pearl waited and waited. She felt as if the Wien airplane was perhaps preserving the woman's body in an icy, silver-gray cocoon. A full moon hung poised in the sky, splashing silver across the wet landing strip. She suddenly recalled a lost memory—a mere flash of a scene she had long since forgotten.

There was a tear in her father's eye when she asked, "Where are you headed with the shovel, Poppa?"

"Old Bet died last night while your momma and I were driving home from Hinton." His voice cracked slightly as he said the words.

"Is that why Momma was riding Morg bareback when ya'll came home?" Pearl inquired.

He gulped back the lump that had formed in his throat. "Yep."

"Does Morg know that Old Bet is dead?"

"Yep. They were pulling the wagon together when she suddenly became ill and I'm headin' out to go bury her."

"Bury Old Bet? Where?"

"Right where she fell." He turned away from his daughter, but not before she saw a lone tear trickle down his cheek. Pearl watched as her poppa balanced the shovel on his shoulder. Then walking side-by-side, he and Morg set out to bid farewell to their old friend, Bet.

Pearl stood, stretched and stared at the stars in the sky. She walked around the aircraft, reaching up to run her finger along the slick, cool metal. She recollected burying her brother Hubert when he was just a newborn, and recalled how guilty she felt about resenting his coming—then when his tiny casket was being lowered into the grave underneath the maple tree. She blinked the tears away.

She thought about Isabel, the woman who had visited her Grandma Dora's when Pearl was a child, and wondered if there was anyone who cared about this Eskimo woman—neighbors perhaps, who would bathe her and dress her in her finest clothes for burial. *What was her name? Does she have children? A husband? Is there anyone who will mourn her loss? I hope this woman has known love in her lifetime, because everyone deserves to be treasured—if only for a short while.*

When the undertaker arrived the following morning Pearl felt relieved of her duty. Exhausted, mentally and physically, she trudged toward her bed praying the Sandman would bring her good dreams by sprinkling magical sand onto her eyes and whisk her away into a peaceful state of unconsciousness.

***

"Miss Bragg!" Frank Whaley waggled his finger. "Could you come here for a moment?"

Pearl walked over to where he was standing beside a tall, young man.

"I'd like to introduce you to Holger Jorgensen. He wants to learn to fly and you're going to teach him."

"Hello, Mr. Jorgensen." Pearl held out her hand.

He shook it tenderly. "It's a pleasure to meet you, ma'am."

"Please, call me, Pearl."

"Okay, and you can call me Jorgy."

"Jorgy," Pearl repeated. "That's a fine name. Please tell me why you want to learn to fly."

"Well," he rubbed his chin thoughtfully, "I took a five dollar ride in a Cessna Airmaster and I was hooked."

Pearl twittered. "That's basically how I got hooked too. It doesn't take much to catch the flying bug."

"For sure." Jorgy nodded, then hesitated. "Ma'am... I mean Pearl, do you have any reservations about teaching me?"

"Do you mean because you are so young?"

His gaze dropped to the ground. "No, I'm referring to the fact that some people don't think Natives are smart enough to fly."

Pearl chortled. "That's the same thing they said about women. Nevertheless," she teasingly winked, "here we are."

He offered a lopsided grin. "Thank you, ma'am."

"Pearl," she corrected.

Jorgy was a natural and Pearl enjoyed teaching him. He was a humble man who had superb navigational skills. It was no time at all until he was ready to fly solo and, although Pearl didn't know it at the time, he would eventually become a celebrated aviator and fly all over the world.

The summer became more interesting when another student, Sgt. Burnaby, arrived. He and Pearl found places to go and things to do. When Victory in Japan came on the 14th of August, they celebrated at the home of their employer, Mr. Whaley, where everyone became quite silly from drinking too much vodka—everyone except Burnaby. Pearl noticed that Burnaby was served far more drinks than she and yet he remained as cool as a cucumber. After the party was over she learned why Burnaby was reaching behind her and dumping his vodka in the window box. You see, in Nome window boxes with colorful nasturtiums and geraniums are kept inside because cold from the high latitude and the Bering Sea breezes would kill them if left outside. A few days later, while they were sitting around swapping yarns, Mr. Whaley suddenly said, "The craziest thing started happening to my wife's flowers after the party."

Burnaby's eyes grew wide.

"Really?" Pearl asked, "What happened?"

"I don't know," he admitted, "but all of Mrs. Whaley's plants have died and she can't—for the life of her—figure out why."

Burnaby shot Pearl a look that she took to mean, "Please refrain from enlightening him."

"Oh," Pearl sighed theatrically, "you know how fickle those nasturtiums and geraniums are."

"Yeah," Mr. Whaley shrugged his shoulders, "I guess so."

Burnaby turned and gave her a quick wink of gratitude.

(Pearl sporting her zootsuit when she was a WASP)

From the Hinton Daily News
Hinton Around

"WHERE ARE THEY NOW?"

After high school graduation Miss Pearl Bragg continued teaching in Summers County and attended summer school at Concord, Morris Harvey, and Davis and Elkins Colleges.

She learned to fly in Bluefield, and was a recipient of Private and Civilian Training Courses at Davis and Elkins College. She served as instructor C.P.T. Course at Marshall University. She served as a commercial Pilot with Instructor Rating, and worked as flight instructor teaching cadets to fly in Charleston and Waynesburg.

Recently, she flew as a Women Air Force Service Pilot (WASP) and is currently working in Alaska as a bush pilot.

PRESENT DAY

By the time we made it through this portion of Pearl's adventures, I felt as though I might burst. I had nibbled on the hot dog, polished off a bologna sandwich, put a dent in the bowl bean soap and scarfed down an entire M&M Blizzard. I figured some caffeine would perk me up, so I decided to order a large coffee to make sure I remained alert.

"I'm going to go get a cup of coffee, do you want one?" I glanced from Libby to Sandy.

"I'll go get us all a cup," Libby offered up.

"Thanks."

"Okay Sandy, Pearl was a cryptographer before becoming a WASP, then after she was cut from the program she immediately went to live in Alaska. Is this correct?"

"Mmm, hmm," she verified.

"She essentially wrecked a plane, hiked up the beach in the Land of the Midnight Sun, then walked for thirteen miles wearing her Eskimo soft slippers," I recapped.

Sandy nodded. "Yes, indeed."

I glanced at my notes. "While in Alaska she saw a fellow WASP friend named..." I flipped through my notebook, "Barbara Robbins, who later married Jon Lindbergh, the son of the famous Charles Lindberg, correct?"

"Yes."

"Then when Pearl was working for Wien Airlines, she had to sleep in a dorm with other men whom she didn't know, and while the male pilots earned a minimum salary, she worked solely on commission." I glanced across the table. "She was a woman living in a man's world, wasn't she?"

"Yes, she was. It was her dream, Dee. Pearl did what she had to do."

"Yeah, I understand. It seems like she had a tough row to hoe."

Libby rejoined us and slid a steaming cup across the table and deposited a handful of plastic creamers on the table. I took a couple sips and shifted the conversation to the man named Jorgy Jorgensen.

"I am not an expert on aviation, but Pearl taught Jorgy Jorgensen to fly. Do either of you know much about him?"

"I know a little about him," Libby replied.

I picked up my pencil and started taking notes.

"Holger 'Jorgy' Jorgensen was an Eskimo born to a Norwegian father and an Alaskan mother. At the time he was born the family lived in the small town of Haycock, which is about one hundred twenty miles east of Nome. He learned how to drive dogs, fish, build skis, boats, and to weld. His father was killed when he was seven years old and he had to help his mother raise and feed his five siblings. He helped by gathering, hunting and fishing for food until he was old enough to work in the mines."

"That is tough work," I interjected.

"Yes it is," Libby agreed. "Then when he turned fifteen he joined the Territorial Guard. By the time the war ended it was hard to fly in the Far North due to the GI Bill and the sheer popularity of flying, but one day he had a chance to take a five dollar ride in a Cessna Airmaster and he was hooked. His mother was furious when she found out he spent all of his money from hauling ice for the winter, but he was so excited that it didn't matter. After his first trip he started taking lessons and met Pearl. He ended up being a noted aviator and flew all over the world."

"He is a legend in Alaska," Sandy added.

"That's an amazing story, and somewhat similar to Pearl's, don't you think?" I asked.

"For sure."

I sipped on my coffee and studied the timeline of Pearl's life that I had brought with me. I tapped my finger on 1945. "Then Pearl ended up in McGrath, Alaska."

"Ah... yes, McGrath," Libby sighed. "Pearl experienced overwhelming joy and a great deal of heartache while living in McGrath."

LIFE IN MCGRATH

From Pearl's experiences she knew there would be no flying in winter, and as much as it grieved her to do so, she gave up September and early October flying for a teaching position and was assigned to the McGrath Territorial School. McGrath's one-room schoolhouse was almost heaven in comparison to West Virginia's schools where she was teaching before the War. There were books, numerous supplies and a two-room apartment in the building for the teacher to live.

Her students were Eskimo, Indian and two Caucasians in grades one through six. Although they were a little better off than her students in West Virginia, she still put a pot of soup or beans on the heater at noontime for anyone who wanted something warm in their belly, like she always did when she was teaching in the mountains. She also quickly learned what a honey pot was—and concluded it was a much better alternative than the thick turds behind the country schoolhouse.

McGrath, a village with an airport runway for its front street, had a population of one hundred forty; half were Eskimo and the other half Indian. Other residents were Civil Aeronautics and Weather Bureau personnel, a few white trappers and business proprietors. McGrath was a village of twos: two saloons, two airlines, two roadhouses, two churches, two stores and two bachelors.

When Pearl went to teach there in 1945, she soon met the two bachelor merchants. Dewey Goodrich, manager of the Alaskan chain store called The Northern Commercial Company, which carried everything from airplanes to casket handles. Dewey was a stocky man with a white mustache, a slight speech impediment, a great sense of humor and an eye for any dame who came by. Due to his round, youthful face it was difficult for those first meeting him to guess his age.

The other store was called Lew Laska's Trading Post, an independent business owned by Lew Laska, a tall slender Jewish man who had come to McGrath as manager of the Northern Commercial Company and later resigned to open his own shop. The two men were friendly competitors, each bent on outwitting the other.

Several times when Pearl stopped in the Northern Commercial store for produce which arrived every Thursday via Alaska Airlines, Dewey asked Pearl for a date. She always declined with the "too busy" excuse. For Thanksgiving he asked her to a chicken dinner at the Slone Roadhouse, where Ma Slone served Ralph's chicken and Dorothy's cake. Pearl reluctantly accepted the invitation. Ralph read a story he had published recently and Dorothy showed her slides of Alaskan scenes.

Once the electrifying entertainment for the evening was over, Dewey invited Pearl up to his apartment for a drink. The store was a large two-story building with the storeroom downstairs and his apartment in the front area of the upstairs. A long hall from the back stairway led to the kitchen and there was a door from the living room to a narrow back stairs used for a fire escape.

Pearl and Dewey went into the living room, where he took her coat and laid it on a chair by the door, mixed a couple of Vodka Collins and brought a plate of squaw candy, which is dried smoked salmon, and two linen napkins with "Mr. Goodrich" embroidered in the corner. Pearl suspected the fine napkins were a gift from an admirer, but he did not elaborate. They sat on the sofa and had a couple drinks. Dewey ran his fingers through his snow-white mustache and purred, "Pearl, if I had a nickel for every time I saw a gal as lovely as you, I'd have a nickel."

She offered him a dubious look.

He tried a more direct approach. "Would ya care for a session in bed?"

"No. Thanks anyway." Pearl carefully placed her goblet on the table. "I should be getting home now."

"Okay." He pondered for a moment. "If you'll wait for a few minutes, I'll shave and then walk you home."

Pearl was more than a bit puzzled about shaving at eleven o'clock, especially since they had just returned from an evening out, but agreed.

"That'd be fine."

She was munching squaw candy and he was in the kitchen shaving when Pearl heard footsteps in the hall—then a woman's voice. "I came to see you, Dewey. So you won't have to come over to my house."

When the woman entered the kitchen, Pearl recognized the voice. She froze. It was that of Rose Peterson. The mother of two of Pearl's students, the president of the P.T.A. and happily, as far as Pearl knew, married to the Deputy Marshall who was now away in Anchorage to testify in an upcoming trial. A nervous laugh tugged at her but she swallowed hard in an attempt to control it. She quickly gulped down her vodka, folded one of Mr. Goodrich's napkins and put it in her bag, along with the vodka glass. She snatched up her coat and slipped quietly out the back door and down the fire escape.

The following Friday, when she stopped in the store for bacon and eggs, Dewey dispensed her change and squeezed her hand tightly. "Thank ya, dear." He gave her a wink. "You are one discreet lady."

***

Lew Laska, in addition to running his trading post, had a riverboat used to haul freight and a small fur factory where parkas, coats with hoods, and Eskimo type footwear called mukluks were manufactured. He had a contract to make fur parkas for Alaska Air Lines stewardesses. Now Pearl, who had made her own clothes for years, even winning a few ribbons in 4-H Club sewing contests, stopped in the store and blushingly inquired, "You're not looking to hire anyone to help you sew parkas by chance, are you?"

"As a matter of fact I am." Lew said pleasantly, extending a hand. "Please, have a seat." He poured her a fresh cup of chicory-laced coffee, making sure he left enough room for cream, and placed it on the old pine trestle table. "Cream?"

"Yes, please."

He slid the silver creamer across the table. "Tell me a little about yourself."

"I have been sewing for years," she told him, as she cupped the steaming mug in her hands, took in the aromatic scent of the strong coffee and added a splash of cream.

"Do you finish projects quickly?" Lew asked, pulling up a chair and plopping down in its seat.

Pearl laughed. "Yes, I do. Actually, I don't mean to brag, but I finished my fourteen-day diet in three hours and twelve minutes."

Lew started to laugh so hard he could hardly catch his breath. "A diet? Why would you be on a diet?"

Pearl giggled. "I was joking."

He pointed at her. "I like your sense of humor."

"Thanks."

"When would you be able to work?"

Pearl drummed her fingers on the table. "After school and on the weekends. I'm trying to save every penny I can earn to buy my own airplane."

"That will work great for me," Lew admitted. "There's always plenty of sewing to be done and I'm always running behind schedule."

It was just then Pearl noticed a black and white Alaskan Husky slumbering in the corner. "Is that your dog?"

Lew glanced over his shoulder before turning his attention toward Pearl. "Yes, he's been my best friend for over ten years now."

"Oh, what's his name?"

"Guess," Lew posed with a grin.

"Hmmm, can you give me a hint?"

"Okay." Lew mused. "He's named after Rip Van Winkle's dog." Lew arched his brow, anxiously awaiting her response.

"Wolf," Pearl playfully barked.

The husky raised his head upon hearing his name and moseyed over to where she was seated.

"How did you know the answer?" Lew asked with amazement.

"Oh," Pearl flipped her hand nonchalantly. "Everyone knows *that.*" She stretched over and rubbed the old dog behind his ear. "Honestly," she glanced at him, "it was one of the questions on my eighth grade graduation examination that I didn't answer correctly."

Lew's boisterous chuckle echoed throughout the store.

"Let me tell you about a recent escapade, Lew."

"I'd love to hear a story." He pointed at her. "Can I pour you another cup of coffee?"

She nodded, shoved her mug toward him and began her tale. "Like my Grandma Dora I am a stickler for cleanliness. Since, as you know, I double for janitor at school I keep the classroom spotless. I came to notice that the students at school were not gung ho when it came to bathing and changing their clothes, so during health class I started emphasizing the need for a clean body and clothes. The health book calls for sleeping with the windows open, but since I can see stars through the cracks in my bedroom at the schoolhouse I assume everyone else has a similar supply of fresh air and won't suffer from the lack of it." Pearl paused for a second to collect her thoughts. "Do you know what, Lew? Since the days are so short now and the temperature is so unbelievably cold, the cracks in my walls are now small glaciers of ice, even the nail heads holding ceiling and wall boards are wearing shiny ice caps the size of marbles."

Lew laughed. "I know what you mean." He pointed to a small frozen crack in the wall behind her.

"Well, last week Tony Shultz barged in, slammed the door and shouted, 'Pearl, damn you! Shut up about bathing! I just came from Pete Snow's house. They had little Peter in a tub of water in the middle of the floor, all their windows and both doors were wide open, and it's forty degrees below zero!' "

Lew broke out in a loud appreciative chortle, smacked his leg and took in a deep breath. "That poor kid…"

"I know," Pearl exclaimed between giggles. "I think I'll skip the health lessons until spring arrives."

"Good idea," Lew agreed, his mouth twitching up at the corner.

Pearl regarded the hefty clock positioned above the front door. "Well, thanks for the coffee, Lew. I better get home." She stood, walked over to the sink and placed her mug down.

"When can you start working, Pearl?"

"Is tomorrow evening too soon?"

"Not at all. I'll see you then."

The very next day Pearl started helping make fur parkas in the evenings and on weekends. She was delighted to have the extra income so she could salt away a few more dollars toward an airplane of her own. It wasn't long until she became an expert in crafting the fur-trimmed parkas.

One afternoon when she was walking from the schoolhouse to Lew Laska's Trading Post she saw a red Aeronca Super Chief with the license NC 31416 in the tie down by the gas pump. *NC 31416. Could it be the Pi I flew years ago? It has to be, because duplicate numbers are never used to identify aircraft.*

She opened the door, dug in the pocket for required logs and there they were—the very entries she had made when she flew Pi five thousand miles away during the war. She was so happy she could have kissed her prop had not the line boy been near by.

"Where's the pilot?" Pearl asked the line boy.

He nodded slightly in the direction of the roadhouse.

She rushed over, opened the door, and searched the crowd for unfamiliar faces. She walked over to the man having a cup of coffee and asked, "Are you the pilot of the red Aeronca outside?"

"Yes, I'm ferrying it to Bethel, which is a village on the Bering Sea."

Pearl smiled. "I'm very familiar with the village of Bethel." She motioned to the chair. "Do you mind if I join you for a minute?"

"Not at all." He motioned to the waitress who brought over another cup of coffee and topped his off.

"Pi used to be my plane." Her eyes sparkled.

"Pi?" he repeated. "Who is Pi?"

She told him about first seeing Pi being pulled from the Kanawha River with her fabric torn, broken wings and splintered propeller, and then about the months she flew the red Aeronca with its less than adequate rigging.

"Why do you call her Pi?" he inquired.

"Well, pi is the ration of a circle's circumference to its diameter. Pi is also an irrational number, which means that its value cannot be expressed exactly as a simple fraction. Since mathematicians can't work with infinite decimals easily, they often need to approximate pi. For most purposes, pi can be approximated as 3.14159 or 3.1416 if you round up."

He stared at her blankly. "Math was not my best subject in school."

"The license number on the red Aeronca is 31416."

"Oh," he drummed his fingers on the table, "I understand... I think."

"Pi in the sky..." Pearl continued to clarify.

"Right," he hesitantly replied.

"Yeah, that plane out there is my old Pi." She enthusiastically expounded, "I found my logbook inside."

He grinned at her passionate declaration. "It's a small world."

"It is for sure," Pearl agreed. "So, why are you taking her to Bethel?"

"There's a trapper planning to use it on his trap line."

"Good." Pearl mulled it over. "I'm glad she still has some life left in her."

From time to time Pearl asked pilots who came the five hundred miles from Bethel about Pi. Months later she was told a storm blew her out to sea. That could have happened but Pearl would rather think Pi flew away to the great airport in the sky.

***

It was in early December when a mild earthquake shook the school building and broke the flue in two places. With no heat the temperature in the schoolroom and apartment soon dropped below freezing. As the children arrived Pearl sent them home with a note explaining the problem and asking for help from any parent. None was forthcoming. As she sat shivering in her parka trying to decide what to do next, Lew Laska, having heard why the children were not in school, came with tools and repaired the flue.

A month later, it just so happened that on New Year's Eve Pearl was partnered up with Lew in a game of Pinochle at one of the local roadhouses. She was not a good player, she couldn't remember what had been played and it was due to Lew's superb skills that they didn't lose their shirts. At midnight the patrons at the roadhouse gathered around the piano and crooned the song, "Auld Lang Syne," and toasted in a new year. Pearl and Lew settled into a corner table and revisited the fateful events of 1945.

"What will you remember the most about last year?" Lew asked.

"Most definitely the end of World War II. How about you, Lew?"

He ruminated on this for a long moment. "I think I'll always remember hearing about the death of President Franklin D. Roosevelt on the radio. I suspect he will go down in history as one of the greatest presidents."

"He did what he had to do for our country, for sure," Pearl agreed. "The only thing we have to fear is fear itself!" she expertly quoted FDR.

"When you come to the end of your rope, tie a knot and hang on," Lew countered.

She pointed at him. "Good one."

"Thanks," he smiled modestly. "I wonder what 1946 will bring."

"Hopefully peace and happiness." She held up her glass and they toasted. "To 1946!"

"To 1946! May we prosper and our dreams come true," Lew added.

Pearl scooted in closer to him so she could hear over the rowdy patrons in the roadhouse. "Tell me Lew, how did you end up in Alaska?"

"Well, I came to McGrath as the manager of the Northern Commercial Company store in 1932 but had a dream of being the proprietor of my own store. I just didn't know how or where this would transpire."

"Wait." Pearl held up a finger. "Where did you live before you moved to the polar region?"

Lew laughed goodheartedly. "I was born in Portland, Oregon in 1898 and when I was three months old my parents moved to Skagway, Alaska, in the midst of the gold rush. Now, the climate of Skagway, along with the tobacco sales that my father was involved in didn't set well with Mother, so they were separated when I was fourteen. Even at such an early age I started earning a living for us. Mother and I lived in Cordova, Anchorage, Fairbanks, then in Dutch Harbor and finally we landed in McGrath. We came to McGrath and I soon started managing the Northern Commercial Company general merchandise store and did well. I was able to save money and make important contacts with wholesale firms in Seattle."

"Why didn't you continue to work for them?" Pearl asked.

"I don't know. I guess around the age of thirty-five I began to make plans for my own business. The local residents were beginning to think about moving across the Kuskokwim River to a new site and I wanted to follow them to the new town. New McGrath offered a better landing strip for the bush pilots, plus the flooding each spring made people think of higher and drier ground. While the Northern Commercial Company was negotiating to buy the Sprague Homestead, I continued with my own plan for a business of my own. I resigned from the Northern Commercial Company and then began obtaining lumber, placing my merchandise orders, and laying the foundation for my store on the bank of Kuskokwim facing old McGrath on land owned by the Naval Reserve."

"It appears everything turned out well for you," Pearl presumed.

"It wasn't easy," Lew admitted. "Once the word was out that I had groceries in Seattle awaiting shipment north, the company used its influence to make sure the freight didn't get shipped from Seattle. I was totally frustrated but wasn't going to quit so I began looking for a way to get my store goods to McGrath. I chartered a boat from Seattle to Bethel but it was sunk during a storm. However, I firmly believed I could do business in this town and take care of my mother. It was about this time I was introduced to a young man from Seattle. His name was Bill Gregg. We ended up combining my assets and Gregg's inherited money and managed to get our merchandise to McGrath. Then in 1938 we opened the door for business." He puffed up with self-evident pride.

"You don't take no for an answer, do you Lew?"

"I'll take on any battle I need to."

"So, what happened next?"

"Our business continued to grow. We had interests in various projects and new inventions. I prompted the United States Postal Service to use my store for the Post Office and started a mukluk factory. I paid seventeen-cents a pound to have a greenhouse flown in from Anchorage to raise fresh vegetables and since I own a movie camera, which takes movies on Kodak color film, I started documenting large fur buys and filming views of my store." He smiled timidly at Pearl. "Am I talking too much?"

"Not at all," she guaranteed.

"I also own a small flat bottomed river boat that can be used for freighting."

"What's her name?"

His confused look did not go unnoticed. "Whose name?"

"Your boat's name."

"Oh," he laughed. "Her name is Vega."

"Vega," Pearl repeated. "It's a nice name."

"Thanks." Lew continued, "Then Mother died quietly at home of cancer in 1943 and I took the somber journey of returning her body to Portland for burial. It was not a pleasant trip."

"I'm sorry."

He nodded appreciatively.

"I haven't met your partner, Bill Gregg. Is he still around?"

"No." Lew shook his head. "His wife grew tired of this small town, left Bill for another man, who happened to be the manager of the Northern Commercial Company store, and Bill took to drinking. He sold me his portion of the partnership and left McGrath."

"That is a fascinating story, Lew. Thank you for sharing with me."

Lew glanced at his watch and realized only the stars in the dim sky had been keeping track of the hours. "Oh, Pearl, I'm so sorry. I've most likely talked your ear off. Do you know what time it is? I should be escorting you home."

***

By spring of 1946, Pearl had completed the school season and set out to buy her airplane. She flew to Seattle and went to the main office of the Northern Commercial Company, where she attempted to persuade them to sell her an Aeronca airplane. Once she was escorted to President Bellingham's plush office she stated her case. "I'm on my way down south to visit my parents and I wish to take delivery of an Aeronca Chief at the factory in Alliance, Ohio."

President Bellingham crossed his arms and gave her a slight nod indicating she should continue.

"It would be great advertising for the company if a woman were to ferry an airplane to Nome," she said with great confidence. Her voice filled the room.

"I can sell anything in Alaska, Pearl." He glared at her over his eyeglasses. "I don't need to advertise."

Her ego immediately deflated.

"Additionally, the factory is on strike and the only two aircraft available are already spoken for. Sorry, but I can't help you."

This was a minor setback for Pearl, however she had overcome many obstacles in her lifetime and this would be another. She would just continue her search. Pearl found a used 1939 Cub Coupe, Piper J4, and flew home to pick up her airplane. Ironically, when Pearl arrived in West Virginia she received a telegram from Mr. Bellingham. He had reconsidered, but it was too late now. Pearl had found her Piper. The only problem she had now was that she was three hundred dollars short of her goal, but Lew wired her the extra money and she was able to buy her own airplane. *Finally!* She was ready to make her way north to Nome, Alaska.

Her Piper purred, ran smoothly in the run-up area, and accelerated down the runway to lift off. At this very moment, she discovered she had the company of a mouse scampering across her feet. The vibrations from the airplane must have startled the little varmint from his slumbering state of bliss and he was scurrying about in confusion. "It's going to be mighty cold when we get to our destination," she told the little fellow. He hunkered down quietly and acceptingly until they made it to Montana. After stopping in Miles City, for a one hundred hour check of her plane, and to find the mouse a new home, she chugged ahead at full throttle.

The stars twinkled like diamonds against the darkening blue velvet sky, and at times the moon looked so dazzling and within reach she felt as though she could caress it with her fingertips. The hours passed as she hovered above the earth, gliding weightlessly in her airborne carrier—dancing in the skies on silvered wings.

Now, one must realize that Pearl had flown through many clouds in her lifetime, facing threatening storms in West Virginia and dark hazes in Alaska, so when she saw a harmless looking cloud approaching she didn't think twice about flying through it. She was immediately buffeted from two thousand feet in the air to two hundred feet above the ground. She quickly learned not to trust dry thunderstorms as she elevated the plane with her heart beating wildly. She started singing to calm her frazzled nerves, knowing that emotions can be raw when soaring with the birds, "I'll be seeing you in all the old familiar places…"

The aviatrix continued on to Great Falls, through immigration and customs and on to Edmonton, Alberta, where she landed to pick up emergency gear and for a briefing. Two other aircraft joined her as the zipped over the newly constructed Alcan Highway. They flew north over Slave Lake and landed in a ball field near Athabasca to refuel. There she met up with a woman named Jean who was a passenger in one of the other two aircrafts.

"Please let me continue north with you, Pearl," she whispered. "I don't have a great deal of confidence in the pilot or the plane I'm riding in. He's been behaving irrationally and I am terrified to ride any farther with him."

Pearl paused before boosting herself into the cockpit. "Who's the pilot?"

"Barber."

"Oh." Pearl thought it all through before reluctantly agreeing. "Well, I was wanting to go it alone, but I don't see why not." She motioned with her hand. "Come aboard."

Some seventy miles out of Fort Nelson, Pearl and her passenger met the Rockies and a raging forest fire. It had blown in from nowhere. Her heart lurched. She had heard horror stories about such fires but wasn't remotely prepared for the spheres of fire leaping from tree to tree. She could smell the smoke but could not see ahead through the stifling air, so she navigated the plane by looking down from her altitude of about fifty feet.

"If I can just stabilize her, we can regain altitude once we clear this smoke." She sounded so sure, so confident. Like one of those chosen few who could survive a plane crash and live to tell about it.

Jean wanted to believe her so she helped by keeping lookout on the right while Pearl watched for trees on the left, and they prayed the pass was no more than five thousand feet so she could get over it. They could see hot blasts scorching the grass of the plateau. Pearl's heartbeat quickened. "Think positive," she admonished herself as she steadied the plane.

The wind seemed to gain strength as the heat of the forest fire increased. The bellowing of the gale and the heavy undertone of the racing flames drowned out the drone of the engine. Jean pointed to a wall of flame rounding the corner of the flat terrain—the edges tinged with flame so they resembled gilded masses drifting across an eternity of space.

"This doesn't…" Jean said something but her words were lost in the vicious gust of smoke-filled wind. Enraged embers rose in the air through the thick veil of fumes. The smoke lifted for an instant and Pearl held her breath as the plane hovered above the blazing woodland. She exhaled deeply when the dense smoke dissipated.

"Wow," Pearl grumbled, noticing her knuckles had turned white, "that was an adventure."

Jean held up her trembling hand for Pearl to view. "I'll never forget it," she said, brushing away the tears copiously cascading down her cheeks.

"Me either." Pearl directed Jean's attention to a slice of clear skies over the divide. The upper strata of clouds drifted on a high current of air and she followed behind them toward the sliver of azure mists far in the distance.

They struggled on until they reached Smith River where they were told that Barber had not reported in. Their charts showed vast areas north of the highway that had not been recorded, and they wondered if Barber became disoriented and perhaps thought those sections were less rugged. They soon learned Barber was presumed lost and a search was under way. There was no news for two days as they waited, but sometime later Barber's aircraft was found although he was never located.

After the nerve-racking journey across the Rockies, both women needed time to decompensate. Jean accomplished this by partying all night with the dame-starved fellas at the Smith River station while Pearl slept the hours away. The following morning, Pearl was sitting in a small booth in the corner of the Dew Drop In Café, drinking coffee, writing notes in her pocket-sized pad of paper, and waiting for her egg and toast to arrive when Jean staggered in the door.

"Jean," Pearl motioned with her hand. "Come over and join me."

Jean had applied makeup that morning to cover the dark circles underneath her eyes, and her long red curls were pulled back in a tight bun, covered by a headscarf knotted under her chin. "Hello, Pearl." She sank into the booth opposite her friend. "Any news about Barber?"

Pearl nodded, took a sip of the bitter coffee that warmed her veins, then added another dollop of cream. "Yes, the news came in this morning. He had come upon a trapper's cabin with his emergency food, and he'd thrown it against the wall in the cabin. Then he took off again and no one knows where he is now."

"He threw his food against the cabin wall?" Jean repeated. "Why?" she stared at Pearl intently.

"Well…" Pearl paused when the waitress approached the booth and placed a plate with scrambled eggs, toast and jam on the tabletop.

The waitress' attention turned to Jean. "Can I get ya somethin', honey?"

"Just coffee."

"Cream?"

"Black, please."

"Do you want anything to eat? I'm buying," Pearl offered.

"Nah, thank ya. My stomach couldn't take it right now."

Once the waitress was out of earshot, Pearl continued, "It is assumed that the mosquitoes drove him mad, because anyone in his right mind would not throw away survival gear or food."

"So true." Jean pounded the table with the palm of her hand. "What did I tell ya? I knew his cornbread wasn't done in the middle." She shook her head. "That fella was as confused as a fart in a fan factory."

Pearl started laughing, fully grasping the old southern sayings. "Where exactly are you from?"

"I hail from Birmingham. Have ya ever been there?"

"Yes, I have. I drove through Birmingham years ago when I went to

Mexico with my sister, Oma, and two other friends."

"I haven't been back since I left," Jean said.

"Any particular reason?"

"Nah, not really." Jean glanced around the café, clearly indicating she didn't want to talk about Birmingham anymore.

The waitress returned, placed Jean's coffee on the table and topped off Pearl's cup.

"Add it to my tab," Pearl told the woman.

"Thanks, Pearl." Jean said, taking a small sip of steaming caffeine. "I will never be able to adequately express my gratitude to ya for allowing me to continue on in your plane. If ya hadn't, I'd been hiking in the snow up to my butt with that odd fella and I'd still be wandering around lost—or worse." She shuddered at the notion.

Pearl chuckled. "You're welcome."

Jean stood, walked over to the other side of the booth, leaned in and gave Pearl a lively hug. "I best be gettin' on to Anchorage. I hope to meet up with ya again someday."

"Likewise. Take care of yourself."

From there Jean continued on to her destination in Anchorage and once again, flying solo, Pearl was ready to venture on. Unfortunately, at takeoff her engine growled, crackled loudly, and sizzled for a few moments before giving up altogether. "Really?" she screamed out in desperation. "What's next?"

She discovered she had lost her chamois skin, used to strain the gasoline, and spent the next day draining the tank of more than half a gallon of rusty water. The following day she was able to sputter on and landed at Weeks Field in Fairbanks, Alaska, then off again to the trade town of Unalakleet.

"Hello, ma'am," an Eskimo greeted as he came to help her refuel her plane, "how was your flight?"

"Adventuresome," she freely admitted.

He laughed, turned around, stumbled and tumbled right smack dab through the fabric wing of her plane.

"Oh no!" Pearl cringed, her hand raised to cover her mouth.

"I'm so sorry, ma'am," the Eskimo apologized profusely. "I'm so sorry."

Pearl took in a deep breath. "I know it was an accident," she kindly responded.

Her mind started churning. A wing on a plane is obviously indispensable, and she needed to find a way to make the needed repair. This ingenious woman, who was raised to be resourceful, found a can of dope glue and with her nail scissors cut out a square from her cotton *Gone with the Wind* skirt, patched up the hole and flew on to Nome.

The aurora borealis dazzled her with its brilliant emerald swirls streaking across the sky as she drifted over the landing strip. It was a luminous vision and she felt as though this brilliant display was sent to personally welcome her home. She waved appreciatively to the skies, set her sight on the landing strip, and even though she had no radio in her plane she imagined hearing signaling coming from the tower.

"Pearl, you cleared to land."

A bright smile formed on her lips. Then with her predictable grace and style—she aced a perfect landing.

***

Pearl returned to McGrath in June and submitted her resignation to the school superintendent. When Lew saw her sauntering down the street he was thrilled.

"Pearl!" he beckoned her. "How was your trip?"

She ran over to meet him. "Lew, it was amazing!"

"Did you talk your father and mother into going for a ride?"

She dipped her chin. "No, Momma said she was sticking with Greyhound and Poppa said he didn't have any reason to be up in the sky, because he hadn't lost anything up there."

Lew laughed and Pearl noticed how the creases in his cheeks deepened to slashes when his mouth turned up in a half grin. She reached out and gave him a warm hug.

"I'm glad you're back home," he whispered.

"Me too."

A month later Lew Laska and Pearl Bragg became husband and

wife. In 1947 their only child, Lewis, was born and soon after Lew began to complain of stomach pain. After a consult with the only local nurse, it was agreed Lew needed surgery and would have to fly to Anchorage. The operation went well but after he returned home the wound site wouldn't heal. They later traveled to Seattle and on to the Mayo Clinic near Minneapolis where he learned he had cancer.

"Pearl, it is my only wish to return to McGrath to live out my time and be buried in the only real home I've ever known and loved."

It was a trying time in the life of Pearl Bragg Laska during the year of 1948 with a new baby and her husband dying, but she was determined to make Lew's final wish come true. Sadly, they were together for only two short years.

Soon after Lew's death, Pearl accepted the fact that she was in big trouble and needed help. Lew's accountant, Bill Head, offered his services in reviewing the books. Pearl left little Lewis with a neighbor and with a load of store records flew to Palmer. Bill went over the books and shook his head. "Heaven help you if they begin to sue." He removed his eyeglasses and placed them on the table.

"I have to try, Bill. I will give it my best."

"Your best bet is to go back, write a personal letter to each of the creditors and tell them of your plans to carry on and explain you will be making payments as early as possible."

"Thanks, Bill. That's what I'll do."

"I also think, if at all possible, you should repay the small creditors each month and send token payments to the large ones."

"Okay."

Back in McGrath she began working up to sixteen hours a day. It is incredible how much one can accomplish with enough motivation. It was the second time in Pearl's life that she was working up to her full capacity. The other time, she recalled, was when she was fifteen and entering high school with a less than adequate elementary education.

Although Pearl missed flying and the income from teaching, all was not lost. In Lew's fur factory she kept busy, first learning to operate the fur machines then changing the patterns to make parkas more appealing to Caucasian customers while retaining the comfort for which Eskimo parkas were so famous. She felt the need to know how each operation was accomplished so she could fill in when a worker was absent. It seemed once a rush order for baby mukluks or a special parka arrived, the Native women failed to show up. *If you want help, look at the end of your arm.* She shifted into a workaholic schedule.

Before Lew had passed away, and being aware his time was limited, he spent hours acquainting Pearl with the business, the riverboat he owned, what they owed and where to find titles and other important papers. There was one he missed or perhaps Pearl was too weary to hear. Shortly after his death, two men, strangers to Pearl, came in the store and asked to see the prospector's drill at the back of the room. Lew had a few gold claims and worked hard one month each year in the spring prospecting for gold. Always one to seek better ways, he had purchased a prospectors drill.

She knew her ship had come in when one of the miners bought the drill for one thousand, seven hundred dollars. She immediately sent five hundred dollars to each of the wholesalers to whom she owed the largest amounts and ordered more groceries and hardware. Her happiness turned to fright when she received a letter from Bank of America telling her they were sending men to pick up the drill on her lot.

The very drill I just sold. Pearl frantically searched through Lew's papers, found nothing, spent a few sleepless nights, and in desperation wired Bill Head asking what she should do. His response arrived the next day by wire:

Not to worry.
I have the bill of sale in my files.
I will be glad to show it to Bank of America.

Demand for her parkas increased. The shops in Anchorage asked for more. A Native lady also had orders for three, so Pearl stitched the "skin sewing" all by hand and worked almost around the clock and was able to make seventeen parkas in November of 1948.

As the year ended she could hardly believe it was gone. Looking back, she missed Lew, and wondered of all people, why she was left alone after such a short and happy marriage. She missed the carefree days of her childhood living up on Chestnut Mountain, where the black mules stand belly deep in the yellow broom sage, and the old women swat at the red wasps in the porch rafters. She contemplated how quickly life changed. Still, she was comforted by the memories and was happy to have little Lewis sleeping soundly with his teddy bear in her arms.

(Pearl in Alaska with her Cessna 150)

CHESTNUT MOUNTAIN
by
Oma Bragg O'Bryan

Way out on the Mountain
To a place called home
Many days were spent
Many days all alone.

How memory still lingers
And stores in a room
All that took place
As childhood slipped too soon.

Now I can return
Anytime, you see
And pick where I learned
Great treasures that God held for me.

Yes, we all know
Changes will come
To us all someday
Yet, quicker to some.

And how I remember
The hours I spent
As twilight came nigh
And fast the time went.

It really isn't sad
As I stop and really see
What memory holds
And brings back to me.

WHERE THE WIND BLOWS

In 1950, the wind blew Pearl to Fairbanks, Alaska, to complete her bachelor's degree at the University of Alaska. While living here she joined the famous Ninety-Nines. This International Organization of Women Pilots was an organization that provided networking, mentoring, and flight scholarship opportunities to recreational and professional female pilots. Amelia Earhart founded the organization in 1929 when she called a meeting for female pilots following the Women's Air Derby. In 1950, Pearl could never have known she would later receive an Award of Achievement from the group, but what she did know was this would help open up opportunities for her as a pilot. There would be Powder Puff Derbies in her future, and invitations to the most spectacular events.

One such opportunity came her way in 1953. It was an invitation to visit London. Pearl immediately picked up the telephone to call her sister, Oma.

In the living room of the O'Bryan's two-bedroom home in West Virginia the telephone rang for the eighth time. "Is anyone going to answer the telephone?" Travis called out as he came in the front door. He plucked up the receiver. "Hello?"

"Hello, Travis," Pearl greeted. "This is Pearl."

"Hello, Pearl. How are you?"

"I'm doing fine. I was just calling to see if I can bring Lewis down to visit with you for a couple of weeks."

"Of course you can," Travis replied. "Hold on and I'll find Oma." He motioned for Libby. "Do you want to talk to Libby for a minute?"

"Sure."

Travis put Libby on the telephone and set out to find his wife.

"Hey there, kiddo! This is your Aunt Pearl."

"Hi, Aunt Pearl. How are you doing?" Libby asked.

"I've been busier than a fiddler in Hades. How about you?"

"I've been trying to talk Mom into trading Sandy for a horse."

"A horse?" Pearl repeated, amused.

"Yep." She sighed. "Hold on a second, here comes Mom."

Meanwhile, Travis found Oma hanging clothes on the line. He said, "Oma, I know you don't like talking on the phone, but it is Pearl."

Oma scurried into the living room and took the receiver from Libby's outstretched hand.

"Hello Pearl." She dropped down onto the vintage wood gossip bench.

"Hey, Oma. How are you?"

"Great."

"How about Travis?" Pearl inquired.

"He's doing fine."

"And little Sandy?"

"She's growing like a weed. How is Lewis doing?" Oma asked her sister.

"He looks like Lew more and more every day, and he's livelier than a puppy with two tails."

"Toddlers are quite active," Oma responded, noticing two-year-old Sandy skipping down the hallway, attempting to hide her sister's doll she was holding in her hand.

"Hey Oma, I was wondering if it would be all right for me to bring Lewis down to West Virginia to stay with you for a couple weeks. I have the opportunity to attend the coronation of Queen Elizabeth the Second and at his age…"

"Absolutely," Oma interrupted her. "We're planning to take a vacation to Daytona, Florida, and he can tag along with us. The girls would adore spending time with their cousin."

"It wouldn't be too much for you? Three young ones can be a handful."

Oma laughed. "Are you kidding me? The more the merrier." She fidgeted with the long telephone cord. "We just found out the Florida

State Agriculture Teacher's Convention will be going on at the same time so we hope to stop at it for at least one day."

"Wow," Pearl clicked her tongue approvingly. "Do you remember how much fun we had in the 4-H club? Didn't we have a blast at the fairs?"

A reminiscent smile wrapped up around Oma's cheeks. "Jackson's Mill was the best."

"Do you visit there often?"

"Not nearly as much as when we were children, but Travis and I are planning to take Sandy and Libby for a visit later this summer."

"Oma, do you remember the day you talked me into swimming across the New River?" Pearl probed.

"*I* talked *you* into swimming across the river? That's not how I remember it. If my memory serves me right *you* talked *me* into it."

Pearl cackled. "I don't think so." Not allowing time for Oma to retort she continued, "Once we made it to the other side we discovered the rocks were as sharp as glass and had to turn around and swim right back." She sighed dramatically. "I was as tired as an old hound dog by the time we made it back."

"Yeah, me too."

"What did you like best about Jackson's Mill, Oma?"

"I don't know," she thought for a moment. "I loved hearing the evening taps in the air, the dining hall and the swimming pool." She paused. "I guess I loved everything about it. My memories of Jackson's Mill are lasting memories."

"Those were the grand old days, that's for sure," Pearl admitted. "Hey, do you recall the time when we formed the social club for the 4-H volunteers?"

"I sure do. Then we borrowed the idea of giving plays from the Barter Theater but admission to our plays was free."

"Yeah, we didn't accept pigs, chickens, fruit or vegetables in exchange for admission like the Barter Theater."

Oma laughed out loud. "Those were the days."

Pearl agreed, "They sure were."

"Pearl," Oma teased, "you must be hobnobbin' with some big wigs to be attending the coronation of Queen Elizabeth."

"Well, it's not as though Elizabeth personally invited me."

"It doesn't matter. It's still a once in a lifetime adventure."

"Very true. I just read that Elizabeth's husband, Prince Philip, has started flight training, so I'm guessing he is a very intelligent man."

Oma laughed at the assumption.

"So, is it okay if we head down to West Virginia next week?"

"Of course, we can't wait to see you and Lewis," Oma assured.

"Thanks, sis. I love you."

"Love you, too." Oma hung up the phone. "Girls!" she called out. "Your Aunt Pearl and Lewis are coming to visit us next week."

Libby started screeching with delight and little Sandy joined in even though, at the age of two, she had no idea why.

A little over a week later, Pearl headed north in preparation for her trip to London and Travis, Oma, Libby, Sandy and Lewis piled in the wood-paneled station wagon for the ten hour drive south to Daytona. Every time a plane flew overhead, Oma would point it out to the children seated in the backseat, it didn't matter if it was a passenger plane or a small, piston-powered aircraft.

"That must be Pearl!" she'd always say.

"Where?" The kids strained their necks, trying to catch even a glimpse of the airplane soaring high above them.

By the time they arrived in Daytona, Travis figured they had crooned, "How Much is That Doggy in the Window?" twenty-four times, "Don't Let the Stars Get in Your Eyes," eighteen times, and the children had squealed through nine questionable sightings of Pearl watching over them from the blue sky. He was a happy man when they finally pulled into the parking lot at the Princess Issena Hotel.

Only two days later, while Oma and the children were playing on the beach and Travis was fishing off the edge of the boardwalk, a tall slender man with sandy-blond hair sat down beside Travis. Their conversation would forever change the lives of the O'Bryan family.

"Are you catching anything?" the man asked.

"Not much. Just a few throwbacks."

The man pulled out his fishing gear and fiddled with the lure. "Are you here on vacation?"

"Yes, I am. I brought my wife, Oma, and our two girls down for some sunshine and I hope to visit the State Agriculture Teacher's Convention for at least one day while we're in Daytona." He pointed toward the beach where Oma was holding little Sandy's hand as she waded in the ocean. "My nephew came with us, too. His mother is in London." He turned and faced the man, holding out his hand. "My name is Travis O'Bryan."

"It's nice to meet you, Travis. My name is Buford Galloway."

"Pleased to meet you."

"So, you're planning to go to the Teacher's Convention, eh? Are you a teacher?"

"I am and so is my wife. We teach in Greenbrier County, West Virginia."

"West Virginia is a beautiful state."

"Yes, it is."

Mr. Galloway informed him, "I'm an educator, too. I'm the principal of Fort White School."

"Is that so? Where's Fort White located?"

"It's in northern Florida." He pulled out some bait and twisted it around the hook. "Where did you go to school, Travis?"

"I grew up in Hix, West Virginia, and attended a one-room schoolhouse until I graduated from the eighth grade. Then I attended high school in Hinton, but the students there aren't too kind to anyone who doesn't live in the town. So, for those of us around the area who traveled by train to attend high school it wasn't always a pleasant experience."

"That's a shame," Buford empathized, "I try to make sure all students feel welcome at my school."

Travis nodded. "It's important for teenagers to believe they belong."

"I agree. Did you finish high school in Hinton?"

"No, I was lucky enough to graduate from Alderson Academy and Junior College."

"Very impressive," Buford acknowledged. "Alderson is quite an expensive school, isn't it?"

Travis chuckled. "I was able to get a job in the laundry room to help pay the tuition. Then one lucky day, I was bouncing down the spiral staircase at the school and the Headmaster saw me. He motioned for me to join him and explained that I had a sponsor. Someone was going to actually sponsor me! I was so excited I nearly passed out. It was a day I will never forget." He turned to face the other man. "I was blessed."

"I would say so. Did you ever find out who your sponsor was?"

Travis shook his head. "No. I never learned who the generous benefactor was, but I could never repay them for the life-changing opportunity to complete my schooling."

"What subject do you teach, Travis?"

"I teach agriculture and I also sponsor the Future Farmers of America."

"Really," a grin wrapped up around Mr. Galloway's cheeks. "Would you consider moving to Florida and teaching at Fort White?"

"Seriously?" Travis twisted around to face the other man.

"I'm dead serious. If you'd come down to Fort White before school starts I can promise you a job teaching biology for the upcoming year then there is going to be an agriculture job opening up the following year."

"Wow," Travis whistled slowly. "Oma would love to move to Florida. Her doctor told her warmer weather would be better for her asthma."

"What does your wife teach?" Mr. Galloway cast his line.

Travis nodded. "Oma teaches home economics."

"I can offer her a job, too. I have an opening for a second grade teacher."

"This is an amazing offer, Mr. Galloway."

"Please, call me Buford."

"All right, Buford. I'll have to talk to my wife about this but I'm definitely interested."

"Why don't you stop and check out the town of Fort White on your way home and let me know what you think?"

"I sure will," Travis answered, the wheels turning in his head.

"Great." Buford presented his minnow-tainted hand and they shook on it. No written contract—their deal was sealed with a handshake.

When Travis told Oma about the unusual and impromptu offer he had just received she was giddy.

"Florida? Move here?" She was so excited she thought she would bust.

"We'll drive through the area first so you can see what you think," Travis suggested.

"I am sure it will be fine, but how are we going to find a place to live with such short notice?"

"We'll figure out the details later, but we can always rent a moving truck that is capable of hauling a trailer."

Libby, who was eavesdropping on the entire conversation, asked, "Are we bringing Brownie with us?"

Oma grinned. "Of course, Brownie is part of the family."

"How will we get him down here?" Libby tilted her head, awaiting her mother's response.

Travis jumped in on the conversation, "We'll build a doghouse that is large enough for a cocker spaniel to ride comfortably, attach it to the tongue of the trailer, and off we'll go!"

"I like this plan," Libby approved.

"Me too!" Oma chimed in.

"Am I moving down here with you?" little Lewis asked.

"No, your mother would miss you too much," Oma tousled his thick auburn hair.

Sandy's eyes grew wide. "Am I moving with you?"

Travis and Oma tried not to laugh but couldn't help but to do so.

"I don't know." Travis rubbed his chin as though he was in deep thought. "What do you think, Oma?"

"I'm not sure..." she teased before sweeping Sandy into her arms. "Of course, the O'Bryan clan *always* sticks together. We are the musketeers!"

Five-year-old Lewis carefully considered this proclamation. "What's a musketeer?"

"A musketeer is a devoted friend," Travis explained.

Suddenly, feeling very sorry for the little boy who never knew his father, he picked Lewis up, placed him on his shoulders, and started galloping around like a horse. "And sometimes musketeers ride horses!" Libby tried not to laugh at how silly her dad was acting, but it was a sight to see. Oma started it first, just a giggle, then Lewis. Then Sandy, who laughed at everything whether she understood what was going on or not, started shrilling with delight. It wasn't long until everyone was laughing so hard they nearly cracked a rib.

That night they tucked the children into one of the double beds and they fell asleep quickly, exhausted from the abundant sunshine, ocean air and exciting events of the day.

"Do you know what, Oma?" Travis didn't wait for her to respond. "If Lewis ever needs to come and live with us he can."

"He is a darling child, isn't he? He is the spitting image of Lew and as sharp as a tack." Oma's eyes smiled just thinking about him. "I assure you, Pearl will always love, cherish and take good care of him."

"I know, I'm just saying if we ever need to..." Travis gave her a wink. "I think the kids are asleep." He motioned toward the tiny couch in the hotel room and whispered in her ear, "Are you in the mood to snuggle?"

His hot breath tickled her ear, sending shivers down her spine. "Snuggle? With you? Hmmm..." Oma grabbed Travis's hand and pulled him close to her. "Anytime, anywhere, Mr. Travis O'Bryan."

***

Pearl stood in the drenching rain with thousands of dignitaries and guests to attend the lavish coronation at London's Westminster Abbey, all the time wondering how Oma, Travis and her darling Lewis were doing in Florida. Once inside, her thoughts turned to the scene unfolding before her eyes. It was nothing short of astounding.

She scanned the crowd hoping to catch a glance of the Duke and Duchess of Windsor, and wondered briefly if the Duke had any misgivings about giving up the throne for love, especially on this particular day when Elizabeth was to be crowned due to his choice. She didn't see them anywhere. *Perhaps they chose to not attend the coronation.*

The ceremony at Westminster was one of pomp and pageantry and the naturally poised Elizabeth delivered, in a solemn and clear voice, the coronation oath that bound her to the service of the people of Great Britain and the British Commonwealth. Pearl paid particular mind to Elizabeth's gown because she had never seen such an elaborate dress. It was made of the finest white duchess satin, richly embroidered in gold and silver thread with the floral emblems of the countries of the Commonwealth at the time. Although she couldn't see the embroidery work up close, she had read that the Tudor rose of England, the Scots thistle; the Welsh leek and the Canadian maple leaf were among the many symbols chosen to adorn her gown. She was attired in full regalia and could not have looked lovelier.

She later learned that the designer, Sir Norman Hartnell, had added a secret detail for extra luck. He included an extra four-leaf shamrock on the left side of the skirt, which was positioned perfectly so Her Majesty's hand would rest on it during the ceremony.

The Return Procession was breathtaking. Colonel Burrows, of the War Office, and four regimental bands, led the parade. Troops from the Commonwealth realms, followed by the Royal Air Force, British Army, Royal Navy and finally the Household Brigade astonished her as they passed with their ornate uniforms and admirable poise. Pearl cheered for the twenty-seven-year-old queen as she passed by her in The Gold State Coach with its gilded painted panels and sculptured tritons adorning each corner. After the Return Procession, she watched as Queen Elizabeth II stood with her family on the Buckingham Palace balcony and waved to the multitude of spectators.

The jet planes of the Royal Air Force skyrocketed above the Mall in a tight, fixed formation and the sheer grandeur of them soaring in precise cadence overhead nearly took Pearl's breath away. She gaped at them in total awe, albeit slight envy. Pearl had heard that the Royal Air Force bomber jets, known as Canberras, were going to fly the film footage across the Atlantic so the Canadian Broadcast Company could air it, and this would be the *first* nonstop transatlantic flight between the United Kingdom and Canada. *Oh, how I wish I could hitch a ride with them.*

***

Meanwhile back in Florida, Oma held tight to Lewis and Sandy's hands as they passed by the craft booths at the Florida State Agriculture Teacher's Convention. The atmosphere put her in mind of the 4-H conventions back home. "Libby! Stay close so I can see you."

Libby stopped, turned around and walked back to where Lewis, wearing a white cotton short sleeve shirt and shorts, was now tugging Oma in a different direction.

"Mom, I'm eight years old. I'll be fine."

"No, Libby, you will not be fine. I want you to stick by my side." Oma gave her the stern "don't sass me" look, prompting Libby to zip her lip and grasp ahold of her younger sisters hand.

"Why did you dress me and Sandy in matching outfits today?"

"Because you look adorable in your two-piece suits, and I can easily pick you out in the crowd since you are dressed the same."

Libby let out a disapproving huff, as they sauntered past the Brahman cattle and toward the picnic tables.

"Stop for a minute, Libby. I want to take a picture of you, Sandy, and Lewis."

Libby reached out for Lewis's hand.

Sandy cried, "No! Hold me."

Oma sighed, tucked little Sandy against her hip and snapped a photo.

Libby instantly released Lewis's hand. "There's Daddy!" She took off running in his direction.

Oma saw Travis, far in the distance, and watched as her daughter snaked through the crowds to where he was seated. She followed behind tugging the two toddlers along in the sticky hot Florida heat. They settled around the picnic table and enjoyed the fish fry, provided by the Florida Ford Tractor Company, and the children went back for several ice cream cones that were furnished by the Florida Dairy Association.

"Isn't it going to be fun living in Florida, Mom?" Libby asked.

"Yes, it is," Oma agreed.

"I wonder if there's going to be free fish and ice cream every day."

"I doubt it."

"Will we be able to go to the beach every day?"

Oma looked at her husband, Travis. "We'll go to the beach *almost* every day," he told his daughter before winking at his wife.

"I like this idea," Libby said, swiping a drip of ice cream from her chin.

"Me too," Sandy chimed in.

"Am I moving to Florida, too?" Lewis asked, for the umpteenth time.

"No, Lewis, your mother will be taking you home with her."

"To Alaska?"

"Uh-hum."

"My mom's at the queen's carnation," Lewis once again explained to Libby and Sandy.

"Coronation," Oma corrected her five-year-old nephew.

"Hey Mom," Libby probed, "do you wish you were with Aunt Pearl in London?"

Oma glanced around the table, admiring her handsome husband, and grinning at the three children whose faces and hands were smeared with the sticky remnants of ice cream—all the time talking her leg off. She heard a vendor in the background, attempting to draw attention to his product, and could smell the distinct odor of cow dung and fertilizer nearby.

"No, Libby, there is no place I'd rather be than right here with *all of you* by my side."

(Libby O'Bryan and Lewis Laska in Florida in 1953)

I NEVER CARED
by
Oma Bragg O'Bryan

I never cared to dance in satin,
Or ride in brocade evening gowns.
I never longed to drive in Spain,
In Portugal, or faraway lands.
I never longed to walk on plush carpets,
Down stately marble halls;
I never cared to dance with kings
At high society balls.
I never cared to ride a Cadillac
Or roam with a chauffeur far and wide;
I never cared to travel the East
Or in the West a camel ride.
I never cared to dress in velvet
Or gold and turquoise, too.
Who cares for beaded jewels?
Or a dress in queenly patterns blue?
I'll take my ride on a mule
And in an oxcart ride,
With my cat and a rooster
And my pets at my side.

PRESENT DAY

I teasingly informed Libby and Sandy, "There is one portion of the Florida trip that you left out."

"Really? What did we leave out?"

"Lewis said that he adored his older high energy cousin, Libby," I replied.

"Did he?" Libby beamed.

"Yes, he said that while he was in Florida he wore sandals for the first time in his life."

Sandy thought this through. "Yes, I guess he didn't have many opportunities to wear sandals having lived in Alaska during his early years."

"So true," I agreed. "Anyway, he said that one day you were romping in a field and he started crying and screaming."

Libby's eyes grew wide. "Why?"

"His feet and legs were on fire!"

"On fire?" Sandy repeated.

"Yep. He was just standing there, minding his own business and the next minute there were red ants covering his feet and legs."

"What happened next?" Libby probed.

"Don't you remember?"

"Vaguely…" Libby cocked her head to the side as though she was trying to pull back the memory.

"According to Lewis, you," I pointed at Libby, "grabbed his hand and rescued him by brushing off his legs."

Both women started laughing.

"I had forgotten all about that incident," Libby confided. "There were no red ants in Alaska for sure!"

"Yeah, that's what Lewis said too."

"Oh, my goodness. I loved Lewis back then and always have. He was like a little brother to me." A lopsided grin covered her face. "I still love him like a brother."

"You were a tightknit family," I presumed.

"Dee, we really are. We keep our families together and always watch out for one another."

Suddenly, the woman I was seated beside of at the presentation approached the table. "Libby and Sandy O'Bryan!" she squealed. "I can't believe my eyes. I was at the Braggin' Rights presentation this morning and learned so much about your family." She signed melodramatically. "I should have asked for your autographs, but I didn't think about it at the time." She squeezed in beside me and plopped down on a chair. "I knew your mother, Oma." Shoving a Dairy Queen napkin across the table, she requested, "Could you make it out to Shirley, Oma's best friend?"

Shirley? My mind started racing. *Just like my Aunt Shirley who propelled her sensual undies and smacked Elvis in the face.*

"Sure, we'll give you an autograph," Sandy inscribed the requested salutation on the paper napkin, signed her name and slid it over to Libby. Libby signed her name below Sandy's and Shirley snatched it up excitedly. "Thank you so much. I'd love to stay and chat but I have so many errands to run." Then as quickly as she appeared she disappeared, leaving me wondering, once again, when it was suitable to chuck a pair of undies at a performer.

I halfway thought I'd share my story about Aunt Shirley with the other women, but figured they'd think I'd lost my mind. So, I picked up my pencil and studied the notes I had written down. "Okay, this brings us up to 1953. What happened next?"

"I think maybe the Powder Puff Derby stories, what do you think, Libby?"

Libby nodded in agreement.

A PERFECT LANDING

During the late 1950s and early 1960s Pearl would fly back and forth between the Lower 48 to participate in Powder Puff Derby transcontinental air races or to take her son Lewis to summer camp.

The first Women's Air Derby took place in August of 1929. While at the time there were seventy United States licensed women pilots, only forty met the race requirements of having one hundred hours of solo flight, including twenty-five hours of solo cross-country, a license from the Federation Aeronautique Internationale (FAI), or an annual sporting license issued by the National Aeronautics Association (NAA).

Of that group, there were twenty entrants in the Derby. Nineteen twenty-nine was also the year the Ninety-Nines Women's Aviation Organization was born, which would enter this picture some eighteen years later. It took eight days to fly the first derby and to navigate the route using only their wits and road maps. Louise Thaden came in first, and fourteen others who completed the race in one of the two aircraft categories were Amelia Earhart, Ruth Elder, Edith Foltz, Jessie Keith-Miller, Mary Haizlip, Blanche Noyes, Opal Kunz, Gladys O'Donnell, Neva Paris, Phoebe Omlie, Thea Rasche, Bobbie Trout, Mary von March, and Vera Dawn Walker.

Although women were not allowed to compete in major air races until the 1930s, many events created separate divisions for them which were identical to the men's divisions, and it was soon noted that the women's flying times were very close to those of the men's. After World War II, one focus of the Ninety-Nines was to revive women's air races. The first of the All-Women Air Race, from Palm Springs, California, to Tampa, Florida, took place in 1947.

The 1948 and 1949 Jacqueline Cochran All-Women Transcontinental Air Race began and would become popularly known as the Powder Puff Derby, which was a reference to the 1929 Women's Air Derby by humorist and aviation advocate Will Rogers.

It wasn't until 1955 that Pearl flew in her first derby.

She didn't win.

It really didn't matter though, because she adored sailing over the morning fog, above the treetops, and into the clouds. An opportunity to fly was all she really cared about so she kept on trying.

"How did you do, Mom?" asked ten-year-old Lewis when Pearl stopped to pick him up where he was staying with a friend.

"We didn't win," she told him, "we landed in Charleston after the deadline."

"That's too bad. Was it because of the weather?" Lewis assumed.

"The weather was not favorable especially when we were flying over Colorado. Eleven planes dropped out because of bad weather, but we plowed on through."

"You didn't quit." He nudged her. "That's what matters the most."

"Exactly," Pearl acknowledged.

"Did Frances Bera win again?" Lewis supposed.

"Yeah, she came in first place."

"Did she fly a Cessna 180 this year?"

Pearl was amazed that her son remembered such details. "No, this year she flew a Beech Bonanza."

"Who was her co-pilot?"

"Evelyn Kelly flew with her this year."

"Really?" He reached over and gave her a hug of condolences. "I'm sorry, Mom. I'm proud of you. Maybe next year."

"Maybe," Pearl grinned. "Hey, Lewis. Have I told you what a great kid you are?"

"Not today."

"Well, you are the greatest kid a mother could ever have."

"You're the greatest mom a kid could ever have."

She held him tight and whispered in his ear, "I think we are just meant to go through this life together."

"Either way, you're stuck with me," he joked.

"Thank God."

Pearl flew in at least one Powder Puff Derby with "Mickey" Michelon, who was a fellow graduate student at Miami University of Ohio, and later several races with Vivienne Schrank. She never won first place in a Powder Puff Derby, perhaps because it is a handicap race, nonetheless she still considered it one of her finest aviation accomplishments and she always aced a perfect landing.

***

In 1963, while Pearl was on sabbatical attending Peabody College in Nashville, Lewis managed to talk his mother into adopting a pet.

"I assure you these chameleons are a pair," the owner of the West End Pet Shop in Nashville guaranteed. He pointed to the one on the right. "That is the male and the cute one on the left is a female." He beckoned for his customers to follow him over to the terrariums. "You'll need to choose one that is big enough for them to have space and privacy," he told them with utmost authority.

"I like this one," Lewis pointed to one on the second shelf.

"We'll take it," Pearl informed the owner.

"Perfect choice." He pointed toward the assorted pebbles and colorful plastic foliage. "Do you know which decorations you want to buy?"

"Decorations," Pearl repeated. "Lewis, I'll like anything you choose."

"And you'll need meal worms, of course," the storekeeper reminded them.

"Of course," Pearl sighed.

With their newly acquired pets and hearty supply of worms, they hurried home, set up the terrarium, with all its trimmings, and watched the chameleons stare at one another until it was time for Lewis's basketball practice and Pearl's Diplomatic History class.

When they returned home, three hours later, they found one chameleon cowering in the farthest corner of their new abode. The other was sitting in the middle blowing up his pink air bubble in the most menacing way.

Pearl waggled her finger at the little fella, "That is no way to treat your future bride."

"Perhaps he has heard how the cavemen treat their women and is giving it a try," Lewis suggested.

"He'll quickly learn it won't work," Pearl promised her son.

Lewis returned from high school the following day with a couple of books on reptiles. "Look," he pointed to a particular photograph, "our chameleons are lizards and from their behavior I'm almost certain they are both males."

The belligerent one was not content to let his adversary crouch in fear. He attacked and before they could come to the rescue the little creature had lost three-fourths of an inch of his tail.

"Any thoughts on what you'd like to name them?" Pearl asked.

"I don't know...."

"How about Lennie and Lizzie Lizard?" she suggested.

"Mom, that won't work. Lizzie is a male."

"So true."

Lewis watched the one-sided battles for a while then chuckled as he taped the names Jonathan and David on the terrarium.

"Why Jonathan and David?" Pearl asked.

"Oh Mom, can't you see how much they love each other?"

"Do you mean like Jonathan and David from the books of Samuel?"

"The very same," Lewis confirmed.

The fights continued, and Jonathan lost another half of an inch of his tail, and David was exiled back to the West End Pet Shop. Regretfully, the situation for Jonathan did not seem to improve. He just sat there and looked sad and sickly. Pearl picked him up by the stump of his tail and set him on the drape by the window. He sat there above the table where Pearl studied him for weeks; growing more emaciated all the time.

Then one morning, while Pearl was trying to solve a difficult statistical problem and thought an extra cup of instant coffee might help, she heated water in a saucepan. She was so intent on solving the statistical dilemma that she spilled some water without bothering to wipe it up. The hot water started cooling as she progressed through the mathematical formula and suddenly she heard a "plop." Jonathan had made a perfect four point landing in the middle of the little pool of water. He relaxed, soaked and steeped in the water. Since he was now enjoying a cleansing bath and a good drink, Pearl decided it would be a good idea to offer him three fat mealworms. He crunched them down greedily.

Each morning after, Pearl put water and worms on the table, while she had coffee and donuts, and they communicated—the way all lizards and teachers on sabbatical leaves do. Then one morning Jonathan saw his reflection in Pearl's makeup mirror and challenged it by blowing a giant pink bubble underneath his chin. Pearl reasoned it was good for his ego to have that mean looking lizard remain coward-like behind the glass.

The lizard became friendlier and would sit on Pearl's arm as she did her homework, and on the nights when the furnace was turned off, the cold-blooded animal sought a warm spot to snooze. Pearl awoke one morning to find him nuzzling against her shoulder, tucked safely beneath the quilt.

"Mom, I like Jonathan," Lewis said, "but I'm drawing the line when it comes to having him as a bedfellow. Actually," he expounded, "I think I'll start closing my bedroom door, and barricade the crack underneath with a pile of towels, just to make sure he doesn't surprise me in the morning."

Jonathan, Pearl and Lewis's unusual lifestyle continued for weeks. Then came spring with gentle breezes, a warm sun and the front door inadvertently left open. They never saw Jonathan again—and he hadn't even bothered to say, "Goodbye."

***

Pearl's 1963-64 sabbatical leave came to an end all too soon and it was time to leave Nashville, Tennessee, for work again in Fairbanks. While she had been in Nashville the United States had experienced a great deal of change and tragedy. The Vietnam War was raging, John F. Kennedy was assassinated, Martin Luther King, Jr., delivered his "I Have a Dream" speech, and the Beatles first appeared on The Ed Sullivan Show. These were events Pearl knew she would never forget. But it was time to move on now and how to make this move required some doing.

While in Nashville, she saw a cute little, neatly furnished Nashua mobile home and the price was right at two thousand, eight hundred fifty dollars. Before considering the logistics of how to get the mobile home from Tennessee to Alaska, she laid down the cash and bought it on the spot.

In early August, the day of reckoning had come. She checked around and soon discovered it would be five thousand dollars to transport it to Alaska. Yes! This cost was along with buying the mobile home and the price of insurance. Pearl fully comprehended that she had a problem. She didn't want to leave her car, airplane or mobile home behind, but something had to be left. She thought her son Lewis, then sixteen, and proud of his job as a counselor at the prestigious Camp Greenbrier in West Virginia, would go along. *Perhaps he can drive the Chevy and I can fly the plane.* She ran the notion over in her mind.

That left only the mobile home and she had misgivings about turning Lewis loose in the car on a long trip. Once before she flew the four hundred fifty miles to West Virginia and let him drive. Pearl wondered what she would do with the hours while she waited for him to drive in the slow car and on the crooked roads.

She had hardly tied the aircraft down and eaten lunch at the Hinton-Alderson airport when Lewis showed up saying, "Mom, I'm starved. Let's order a couple of hamburgers."

"Sure." She motioned to the waitress.

"Lewis, I've been thinking this through and if I take the airplane to Fairbanks it will be so cold and dark so I won't fly it much. Then every time a heavy snow comes I'll have to rush to the airport to sweep off the wings. I don't really need it, do I?"

"It's up to you, Mom." Lewis gobbled down his burgers.

She drummed her fingers on the table, deep in thought. "I'm hoping to make some money on the mobile home and I won't get it if it's sitting in Nashville."

"True," Lewis took a long satisfying drink of his sweet tea.

"Why don't I take it up north myself?"

"You could…"

"Right! I can if I want to."

Consequently, Pearl went over to Colemill Flying Service, rented a hangar space for twenty dollars a month for the airplane with the privilege of parking the 1958 Chevrolet under the wing. Then with truck advertisements in hand, she went to Capital Chevrolet and found a close model year and bought a new four speed three-quarter ton pickup truck, paid to have a good hitch installed and found an authority on trailer hauling.

"Look Jerry, I'm afraid of controlling the mobile home brakes with a lever on the steering wheel. I've seen too many jackknifes down steep hills on the Alaska Highway and I don't want to end up in a messy situation."

"Well, Pearl, I could integrate the mobile home electric brakes with those of the truck, that way pressure on the truck pedal will also brake the mobile home."

"Thanks, Jerry. I believe it will work."

"It will," he replied with certainty.

Her next chore was to call Lewis at the camp and explain to him how and why they were ready to be on their way to Alaska. "It's a wonderful plan," she told him, with more confidence than she felt.

"Oh, Mom, what next?" He fully comprehended what the hushed silence on the other end of the phone meant. "I'll talk to Mr. Garnett and call you back."

Later in the day, Pearl dialed him up. "Hello, Lewis. What did you find out?"

"Honestly, Mr. Garnett thinks it would be bad for camp morale if counselors begin taking off two weeks before the close of camp." He continued, "Bill Wade, the Bear's football player, or John Havlicek, the basketball great, who were counselors in their youth would never have done such a thing."

Although Pearl had a sinking feeling in her chest, she said, "I understand, Lewis. I'll make out just fine. You stay until the camp closes and for the house party if you need to, then you can catch the Greyhound Bus to Seattle and from there get a flight on Pan Am Airlines to Fairbanks."

Pearl parked the car, loaded Lewis's and her personal things, including his target pistol and 22 rifle in the mobile home and even though she was scared stiff, she took off at daybreak on Route 41 for Chicago. She had no idea how wide turns should be to clear corners with her fifty-three foot cargo. In small towns, with little traffic, she experimented until she knew fairly well how to make the turns.

Darkness caught up with her just outside Chicago, and she had traveled four hundred forty-five miles when she pulled into a massive truck stop, ate supper, crept into the mobile home and slept fitfully until four o'clock in the morning. At the first hint of daylight she was on her way. The traffic for the next thousand miles was enough to cause gray hair, and Pearl was as nervous as a long-tailed cat in a room full of rocking chairs while navigating through the multitude of vehicles.

Minneapolis, St. Paul was next and she dreaded it like the plague, but luckily she made the four hundred miles on Route 12 in time to get through before evening rush. She took Route 10 to Detroit Lakes, Minnesota, where she changed to 59 North to the Canadian Border. At near dark she stopped at a truck stop south of St. Cloud and gassed up, ate and slept better. With Nashville, Chicago and the Twin Cities behind her in two days, she had driven only nine hundred miles, but they were hard ones and she felt satisfied. All that remained was the Alaska Highway and like Scarlett O'Hara she told herself, "Tomorrow is another day!"

Since mobile homes were not permitted on the highways after dark or on weekends in the United States, Pearl had only three days to travel before she would have to stop for the weekend. *If I can only make it to the border I'll be home free.* She had good luck and good winds and made the border at two o'clock in the afternoon. She figured she could clear customs and knock off a few miles in Canada before dark.

She didn't.

Lewis's target pistol was the fly in the ointment.

They had taken it through Alaska clearing customs and immigration in Great Falls, where they merely sealed it and then showed it wrapped-up at the Alaska border. Not so here. No way could Pearl take it and there was nothing to do but go downtown, have it wrapped and shipped by Railway Express. This took up what was left of Friday. *Oh well, I'm in Canada now and can travel tomorrow.*

Saturday morning, she was so relieved to have successfully come through the United States that she stopped at a campground outside of Winnipeg and treated herself to a shower. Dark eventually caught up with her but she was feeling better all the time.

Sunday was another story. She encountered strong north winds and made poor time. She was getting five miles to a gallon of gasoline. The going was so slow that half the day was gone when she reached Edmonton. Yet, the wind died down and she reached Dawson Creek, B.C. at dark. On Monday morning, she watched as the sun fully peeped out from behind its cloud cover, sending rays of brilliant light through the parting trees. Today would be spent getting the truck serviced, bubbles put over the headlights and the mobile home taped to protect against flying rocks and gravel. She shopped for her annual supply of goodies like Doukhobor jam and Canadian bacon and she was fourth in line to have her truck checked. The other outfits, she noticed, were taking on half a dozen spare tires. A fella approached her as she waited and asked, "Are you traveling to Alaska?"

"Yes, I am."

"Where's your driver?"

"I am the driver." She squared her shoulders.

"Do you suppose you have enough tires?" he queried.

Pearl nodded. "I have a new spare on the truck interchangeable with the mobile home."

He shook his head skeptically and went on loading tires.

Pearl later saw the same fella while she was rolling down the road around Summit. The hood of his rig was unbolted and dense steam was gushing from the engine—forming foggy smog as it dueled with the chilling northern temperatures. Naturally, she honked the horn, offered him a gesture with her hand, and then waved goodheartedly as she breezed on down the highway.

Up the Alaska Highway she kept a steady thirty-five mile per hour speed limit, only stopping for gasoline, to eat or until she was utterly exhausted. On Thursday, the eighth day out of Nashville, with her truck and mobile home caked with dust-covered mud she pulled into Fairbanks. She was fortunate to have had no flat tires. The only damage was a crack in the truck's windshield from a flying rock and a broken holding tank in the mobile home bath. She had heard it break when she hit a frost boil after reaching the paved road in Alaska.

A couple of weeks later, when she drove to the airport to pick up Lewis, his remark was, "Mom, I'm sometimes proud of you and other times your hair-brained stunts are downright embarrassing. When will you bring another mobile home up the highway?"

Pearl smiled, but thought to herself, never again—no never in a million years.

In her desire to forget, what Lewis had called her hair-brained stunt, she never looked into the profit or loss results of her mobile home adventure and did not determine if she made any money. But, all in all, she drove four thousand miles in eight days, with an average of nine and one half miles per gallon of gasoline and in the end Pearl's costs were as follows:

Gasoline and oil = $234.00
Bubbles and tape = $27.50
Toll Roads and bridge = $12.00
Garage (Lube) = $16.50
Insurance = $53.00
Shower at campground near Winnipeg = $1.00
Meals = $47.50
Total = $391.50

Pearl used the truck for one year and sold it for one thousand, eight hundred dollars and as for the mobile home, she kept it for seven years, living in it for five of those, and eventually sold it for three thousand, five hundred dollars.

"*Perhaps,*" she decided, "*I made out fairly well on the long haul.*"

(Later, All-State Insurance sent her a refund and cancelled her insurance, but she no longer needed it—she was already safely in Fairbanks.)

***

It was in 1972 that Pearl left Alaska to care for her elderly parents, Johnny and Laney Bragg. Meanwhile, she continued to pursue her passion of flying. When J.E. Faulconer, a reporter for the Hinton Daily News, learned that Pearl Bragg Laska had returned to Summers County to take care of her father and mother, he telephoned to request an interview.

"Sure J.E.," Pearl warmly consented, "when would you like to come over?"

"Anytime really, will next week work for you?"

"No. I'm driving to Alaska next week in my camper van," Pearl explained.

"Driving? All the way to Alaska?"

Pearl laughed. "Yes, I have twenty-four Alaskan fur trimmed parkas I've made and need to haul them up north. They sell for about a hundred eighty dollars each and that's how I earn a little extra money in the winter months."

"Oh," J.E. replied, the disappointment recognizable in his voice. "Is tomorrow too soon?"

"It will be perfect. Stop on by in the morning."

"Thanks Pearl. I'll see you tomorrow."

J.E. had known Pearl some thirty years earlier and had written about her feats as a pilot in the Powder Puff Derbies in which she raced, but other than that he hadn't kept up with his old friend. Subsequently, on the following morning, J.E. made the drive to Pearl's Elk Knob home, positioned on a high plateau overlooking Bluestone Dam, and pulled alongside the immaculately kept ranch-style home where he saw his old friend standing on the porch waving at him when he jumped out of the car.

"Hello, J.E.," Pearl motioned for him to come inside. "How have you been?"

J.E. reached out and gave Pearl a hug. "I've been fine. Thank you so much for agreeing to talk with me."

"Come in and let me brew you a cup of coffee."

J.E. followed Pearl through the cozy living room with sizable windows overlooking the mountains and into the kitchen. J.E. watched as Pearl quickly rinsed the filter basket, spooned in enough grounds for a pot, and continued to fill the carafe with water. "Please have a seat."

J.E. pulled out a chair, plopped down on it and began to explain his hopes of interviewing Pearl about her life to publish in *Hinton Around* as a human-interest story.

"Uh-hum," Pearl poured them both a cup of coffee and slid the steaming cup across the tabletop. "Ask me anything, and I'll tell you what I remember."

"Okay, let me see…" J.E. pulled a notepad and pen from his attaché case. "You have been piloting airplanes for forty-three years now, and at the age of sixty-six you must be one of the oldest pilots in the country, wouldn't you say?"

"Sixty-seven," Pearl reached over and gave J.E. a spry pat on his hand, "and it is possible that I am one of the oldest pilots still in the air."

"I know you used to own your own plane. Do you have one now?" J.E. asked, running his fingertip around the edge of the cup.

"No, several years ago I sold my plane to Ruth Gwinn who operates the Pence Springs Airport. But occasionally I borrow it to fly to New York to get supplies to make my Eskimo parkas, and I'll sometimes fly to Nashville to visit with Lewis." Pearl puffed up. "Lewis is an attorney in Nashville. He's a smart young man and the spitting image of his father, Lew."

J.E. wrote down a few notes to help jog his memory later. "Along with being a pilot you are also a teacher, correct?" He glanced at her. "If I remember correctly you've taught for years but I want to make sure I get the details correct."

"I understand." She offered him a teasing wink. "Yes, I love teaching. You know, J.E., I didn't start school until I was ten years old and seven years later I was teaching school."

"I didn't know that," J.E. admitted, as he flipped through some pages of notes he had jotted down earlier. "I heard you had come home to care for your parents and now that they have passed on over to the sweet by and by, do you plan to stay here in Summers County?"

"I'm not sure…" Pearl rubbed her chin thoughtfully. "My mother, Laney, died last June at the age of eighty-eight and my father, Johnny, died in August at the age of ninety, so right now I'm settling up their business and caring for their graves. They are buried up on the farm they used to own so I mow the grass and make sure everything stays tidied up at the cemetery. In fact, last week when I was up there my car got stuck in the cattle guard rails at the gate and Mr. Gwinn and his wife came by and helped me get unstuck. You probably know the Gwinn's bought the old homestead."

"Yes, and it is a prime piece of property. It's beautiful up there." He scanned his notes again. "Pearl, how did you learn to fly? I mean, it wasn't a common career path for women, especially back in those days."

"Ernie and Harvey taught me to fly at Bluefield when I was twenty-four, then I received my commercial pilot's certificate and was teaching school and flying when Pearl Harbor started World War II. I resigned from teaching and went to flight instruction for the government during the war."

"How did you end up moving to Alaska?"

"One day in 1944, a woman pilot flew in, ferrying a plane some-where, and she told me that Alaska was the place for big opportunities in flying. She said they were crying for bush pilots up there."

"You just packed up and went?" J.E. asked disbelievingly.

She could remember it as though it had occurred yesterday. "It was the way the wind blew me. I grabbed the next plane to Alaska and flew to Fairbanks. The fella running the bush line wouldn't hire me, but told me to go to Nome where they really needed pilots. He said if I made it for a year in Nome, he'd hire me."

"Obviously you made it."

"I did. I went to Nome and was flying the next week. Oh, wheels in the summertime and skis in the winter of course. Flying in West Virginia had provided me with the perfect background for flying in Alaska." Pearl glanced at J.E.'s coffee cup. "More coffee?"

"Yes, please." He pushed his empty cup across the table.

"It wasn't too long afterwards that I flew into a community called McGrath and met Lew Laska. He was the love of my life and, as I'm sure you know, we later married."

"I've never heard of McGrath," J.E. admitted.

"Oh, you are not alone. Most people haven't heard of McGrath. It's kind of like explaining where Chestnut Mountain is located." Pearl laughed. "McGrath is about two hundred miles northwest of Anchorage and about halfway to Nome."

J.E. wrote the information down in his notebook, took a sip of coffee and asked, "When did you marry Lew?"

"It was in 1946. However, Lew died two years later leaving me with my handsome son and a ready-made business and trading post. Lew taught me how to make fur clothing and ultimately I became quite an accomplished maker of fur parkas, if I do say so myself."

"What are parkas made of Pearl?" He leaned in and whispered, "I heard they were made of seals, is it true?"

Pearl nodded. "Yes, seals, beaver and wolverine."

"Really?" J.E. scratched down a note. "Will you show me one of the parka's you've made?"

"Of course! Let me go grab one."

A couple minutes later, Pearl returned and explained, "Today, they're made of fake fur and trimmed in wool, with real leather trim. I got the pattern from an old Eskimo woman in Nome a long time ago. So it is authentic Eskimo."

"It's very attractive," J.E. ran his hand over the soft material.

"The bird on the trim is the Ptarmigan."

J.E. wrinkled his brow in thoughtful repose. "How do you spell Ptarmigan?"

Pearl indulged him with the correct spelling. "It's Alaska's State bird."

"I see." J.E. wrote it down. "That makes sense."

"Years ago, I made the parkas of real skin and fur, but of course, it has all changed now. I sell them to an outlet in Fairbanks, and they sell them to tourists."

"What do they tell the tourists about where the parkas are made?"

"Oh, they're made by the Eskimos in Nome, of course!" Pearl told him with a chuckle. "I've also started making Tundra Patch Kids," Pearl confided, "but I don't quite have them perfected yet. They are cute dolls dressed in parkas."

J.E.'s jaw dropped in amazement. "I want to buy one for my wife when you start selling them."

"I'll add you to my list," she teased.

J.E. burst out laughing. "Thank you." He studied his handwritten notations. "Let me recap. Lew taught you how to make parkas... and after he died you most likely had a lot on your plate," he recited out loud. "How did you manage after your husband died?"

"It wasn't easy. I continued running the business, went back to teaching school and kept up my bush flying. Since there are no roads into McGrath there was always plenty of work available for pilots."

"And you managed to raise a successful son," J.E. added.

"Yes, I did. Lewis is the joy of my life. I'm very proud of him." She got up, walked into the living room and returned with a portrait. "This is Lewis," Pearl said as she showed J.E. the photograph of her handsome son.

"You have a good-looking boy, Pearl. So, this is what Lew looked like?"

"Very much so." Pearl settled back down into her seat.

"What happened next?"

"Well, meanwhile I entered the Women's Transcontinental Air Race in 1955, and flew my fifth race in 1961."

"The Powder Puff Derbies, right?"

"Uh-hum. However, I never won," she sighed melodramatically.

"Was it worth it?" J.E. asked, polishing off his coffee in a single gulp.

"Oh, heck yeah! It was the most flamboyant of my many interests, especially in the world of women's flying."

J.E. stared across the table at Pearl. "You have led a most interesting life," he told her sincerely.

"It's been a ride," Pearl admitted. "I'm just hoping that when the time comes, I make a perfect landing."

"I have no doubt you will," J.E. smiled as he closed his notebook and tucked it back into his attaché. "Pearl, how is your sister, Irene, doing? I haven't seen her for quite a while."

"She's doing great. She is a teacher and her husband, Linus, works for the railroad."

"Good. She was always a sweet girl."

"She's smart, too," Pearl added.

J.E. nodded in agreement. "Thanks for taking the time to talk with me." He stood up and was about to leave when he turned and asked, "Have you seen Marion O'Bryan since you've been home?"

"Marion?" A grin wrapped up around her cheeks. "In fact, Marion and I have spent some time cataloging the cemeteries around this area."

"Really? It is a worthy undertaking and it certainly needs to be done before the headstones collapse at some of the older sites."

Pearl nodded. "We thought so too. My niece, Sandy, wrote a short story called *The Chestnut Mountain Home*, and when I was reading it last month I came across a little tidbit I didn't recall." She rummage through some papers stacked on the table. "Here it is. Let me read this part to you." Pearl laid the paper flat on the table and began reading aloud:

"As the family grew, another bedroom was added, and the porch and current kitchen was built. The barn on the hilltop was still there, but John needed a second one. It is up on the hill where Mr. Jaseon is buried alone. John fenced in the grave so the cows wouldn't bother him. There were lots of stories about him. They say he had been married four times, and that he didn't like any of his wives very well. He said they talked too much. Of course, that is just gossip. I wasn't here then. The tombstone says, 'Elmer Zek Jaeson, 1823-1901, May he rest in peace.' I suppose he's peaceful up there by himself!"

Pearl laughed out loud. "It made me start wondering how many graves like Elmer's are up here on this mountain, which is when the idea of cataloging the cemeteries and graves came to mind. Marion said he'd help me and we've been visiting different sites since then." She paused before confiding. "J.E., did you know I had the biggest crush on Marion when I was a teenager?"

He laughed. "I did not." His brow arched mischievously. "You do know Marion is a widower, right?"

"Oh, hush up." She flipped her hand dismissively.

"All I'm saying is…" he winked.

Pearl gave him a warm smile. "Stop by anytime, and bring your beautiful wife with you."

"Will do." J.E. promised.

(Pearl running to validate her time card in an early Powder Puff Race)

LADY OF THE BLUE SKY
by
Oma Bragg O'Bryan

All hail thee, pert Girl
A Nomad with courage,
Steering through windy hurls
On that dubious pilgrimage.

Soaring higher out and on
A Trojan Girl thou art,
With all weakness gone
Victory from the start.

Thou sea-bar of the mighty
Native of the skies unknown,
Mistress, lover of the unlikely
Exceled all a fear of storm.

Daring lady of the blues
Lonely as a bird in love,
Lifts her wings high o'er gray hues
This mighty girl who flies above.

BRAGGIN' RIGHTS

California was *the* place to be in January of 1981. Ronald Reagan succeeded Jimmy Carter as the 40th president of the United States and minutes after he took office, Iran released American hostages thus ending the four hundred, forty-four day Iran hostage crisis. Pearl was relieved to know that she, like Americans everywhere, would no longer need to worry about the fate of those who remained from the original fifty-two men and women held in captivity.

She had recently moved to Riverside, California, to be close to her sister Pauline and it was here that she met and married her second husband, Ed Chamberlain, at the age of seventy-five. Since she had sold her plane while caring for her parents in West Virginia, she rented a Cessna 150 and crafted two special pillows to help boost her visibility while dancing with the clouds. She also joined the local chapter of the Experimental Aircraft Association and a group called the Flying Octogenarians.

"Hey, Pauline," Pearl posed, "would you like to go with me to the Ninety-Nines convention?"

"The Ninety-Nines," Pauline repeated. "Does it matter that I'm not one of them?"

"No." Pearl shook her head. "We'll have fun and you'll hear some great stories about flying."

Pauline shrugged her shoulders. "Why not? Where's it at?"

"The Anchorage Sheraton."

"I'm in."

"Great." Pearl motioned for her sister to follow her down the hallway of the cozy two-bedroom apartment. "Look what I've been making for the convention." She opened the door to the spare bedroom where Pauline saw hundreds of lapel pins covering the blue and yellow patchwork quilt adorning the bed.

"These are amazing, Pearl. How many did you make?"

"Eight hundred."

"Excuse me," Pauline cleared her throat, "did you say eight hundred?" She felt tired just thinking about how long it would take to fashion one of them.

"Yeah, it only takes me about an hour to make one."

The little Eskimo buttons looked as though they were wearing a parka with soft, fluffy fur surrounding each of their cute hand-painted faces. Pauline picked one up and examined it carefully. "You constantly amaze me, Pearl. These are stunning."

"Thanks," Pearl replied modestly, "I made them for the Amelia Earhart Luncheon."

Pauline carefully placed the brooch back in its proper place. "I see. Besides being an experienced aviator, you have imagination, ingenuity and above all, stick-to-itiveness."

Pearl laughed. "Oh yeah, I'll stick to it until the last pea is out of the pod."

"Well, I want one."

"You'll get one at the luncheon," Pearl joked.

Pauline had a blast at the convention and eventually wrote an article for *The Senior Tribune* about her adventures hobnobbing with the famous women aviators in 1984, and it went something like this:

> I thought teachers had a monopoly on talking about their profession. I was dead wrong. I attended the International Convention of Ninety-Nines, Inc. held in Anchorage, Alaska. The convention was open to the public and I wanted to be there because my sister was being honored, because she was one of them—I wasn't.
>
> I stood in line at registration and thought for a minute I could be in a Car Care course in an Adventures in Learning class sponsored by the Life Enrichment Services. Words like engine and grease fell freely from their lips. Alas! The words airplane and aviation history didn't fit. I decided my best alternative was to listen—there was no way my conversation could be faked to make me one of them. They were in. They understood the fine points of aviation,

they knew the craft well, they were experienced aviators, and they had flown the rough skies.

They were talking about float plane flying as well as mountain and glacier flying along with landing on all kinds of beaches, hard packed sand, soft sand pebbles and even rougher terrain. No, I wasn't one of them! I have landed by commercial plane in the midst of an extraordinary group of experienced women aviators who not only love to fly but also like to talk aeronautics with the technical understanding of their Forty-Nine-and-a-Halfers, as their flying husbands are called.

If you have been thinking this must be a youth oriented group and all the aviators are young, you are wrong again! I saw plenty of snow on the mountain. From observation and statistics, their flying spans some fifty years or longer. Some of these veterans received their pilot's certificate in the twenties and thirties with others getting their licenses in 1984. Buffy Bush probably the most recent pilot at the convention, having received her license this year. Look at the years. Imagine, Pearl 1934, Buffy 1984. Incredible again! I tried to recall how I looked at Buffy's age, but dismissed the thought—too many years behind me.

Amelia Earhart organized the elite group of Ninety-Nines at Curtiss Field in New York in 1929. She was the first president of the group of ninety-nine licensed pilots. Miss Earhart encouraged women to become aviators. She said back in the twenties and thirties, "If enough of us keep trying we'll get someplace."

Imagine, if you can, Amelia Earhart at the Anchorage Sheraton registering along with eight hundred women aviators, 1984 style. The women aviators in attendance winged in from nineteen countries, Australia, India, Israel and other along with air pilots from forty-six of the United States, and I had to ask myself, "How did I get to be in the midst of them?"

***

On Pearl's ninety-fourth birthday, she received a letter from her son

Lewis, now an attorney and college professor in Nashville. It read:

April 24, 2003

Dear Mom,

{After our conversation early this week, I wanted to let you know that I remember the day you mentioned very well.} It was winter, cold and dark and it had snowed. You insisted that I go and help you sweep snow off the wings of the Cessna 150. I didn't want to go and I was resentful that you had spent all that money on something that you didn't use except in the summer. I was grumpy. Putt, putt went the car as you carefully drove to Phillips Field. We got out of the car and I realized I had to do the manly thing and wade in waist-deep snow to clear the wings. The job done, we started back. On the way back, I saw something that I had not seen in my grumpy mood getting to the plane. I saw the saddest sight anyone could ever see. Two planes, both fabric-winged Pipers had collapsed wings. They looked like badly injured birds. Suddenly I realized something. "Mom takes care of her airplane and she takes care of *me!*"

You are now and have always been the very best Mom anyone could hope for and you will always be first in my heart.

Love,
Lewis

P.S. Please stop complaining about not having much energy. You are only 94 years old, for Pete's sake! Plenty of flying hours left!

***

Pearl's son was certainly correct when he stated she had plenty of flying hours left, because at the age of ninety-four she passed the physical to renew her pilot's certificate. Although the child was grown the dream was not gone. She flew up in the clouds over the blue-gray Appalachians passing over Chestnut Mountain where she had grown up. She circled around and followed the New River, its far bluffs looked blue in the distance, they were flat-topped and covered with dark, dense forest and brilliant cerulean-green meadow grass, and then she set her sight on the landing strip and once again aced a perfect landing.

On her one-hundredth birthday, which was April 29, 2009, Pearl was pleasantly surprised when she received a note from her fellow aviators in Fairbanks, Alaska, displaying this heartwarming greeting:

"There is no other pilot maneuver that demands the full test of skill, depth perception, judgment, experience and alertness than the final approach to landing. Anyone can fly an airborne plane.

On final, like life, it is the last act before termination of flight. I know of no other joy that I have had than the thousands of final approaches I have made, each time trying to make it better than the last. The pure joy of command and flying that aircraft on final is the pilot's report card.

I am on the Final Approach of my life. I have little regrets, I have had thrills and experiences and I am pleased to hear the tower when they say, 'Pearl, you are cleared to land.' "

Pearl Bragg Laska Chamberlain
1909-2012

At the age of one hundred three, Pearl Bragg Laska Chamberlain made her final flight and one can only presume—aced a perfect landing.

PRESENT DAY

I glanced at my watch and wondered if Libby, Sandy and I were going to be kicked out of the Dairy Queen soon, since we had been occupying the table for over three hours now.

"Libby and Sandy, I can't thank you enough for taking time to talk with me about Pearl's adventures. I believe I have everything I need to complete *Pearl: You are Cleared to Land*. Lewis sent me two stories I am going to include and I think I'll add a brief description about my flying lesson."

"Lewis sent you stories? How exciting!"

"Yes, he also said that at the age of eighty, Pearl took up flying ultralight planes. They were not to her liking because these planes could not fly very far, only an hour or so at a time." I pulled out a photo to show them. "Here she is standing by an ultralight."

"I've never seen this photo, have you Sandy?" Libby passed it across the table.

"No, I don't think so." She handed it back to me and I tucked it safely back into my notebook.

"Well, I appreciate you taking the time to talk with me and for sending me her stories, and the newspaper articles… and everything." I stood and stretched my legs. "I'll send you the manuscript as soon as I'm finished so you will have time to read through it and correct any facts that I may not have recorded correctly."

"Thank you, Dee," they chimed.

"No, thank you. I am honored to have met your family."

***

Below are the two delightful stories Pearl's son, Lewis, sent to me about flight experiences he vividly recalls.

A Take-Off at Northway
by
Lewis L. Laska

The Alaska Highway was not built for people travel. It was built for airplanes. Running mostly through Canada, it was not built by Canadians, not an inch. Furthermore, black U. S. Army soldiers built it. Two large construction battalions ("CBs") had worked at breakneck speed to build the road from Dawson Creek, British Columbia to, well, Fairbanks. As late as 1972, when Mom and I drove it to the Lower 48, it was still an unpaved, gravel road. Some of the black men had stayed in Fairbanks.

The Highway was merely a way to build airports for fighter planes and bombers to get to Fairbanks during the war. There, or sometimes at Nome, the Russian pilots would pick up the planes and fly off into eternity. Some of the Russian pilots were women, but they were not allowed to pick up the planes. Just fly them and get shot down.

Meanwhile, in the United States, women pilots (called WASP's) for Women's Army Service Pilots, were allowed to ferry planes from the factories, but were not allowed to fly them in combat. All this was well known by 1944 when my mom, Pearl Bragg, left WASP training and went to Alaska to become a bush pilot, flight instructor, and public school teacher. But that was long ago.

Flash forward to late August or early September 1964. We had left the Lower 48 in Mom's Cessna 150 a few days before, but unlike most trips, we had a deadline. She had just completed courses at Nashville's Peabody College in a new field called special education. She had to get her transcript approved in order to get a pay raise before the school year started back in Fairbanks. No exceptions, no excuses. We had to be in Fairbanks by a certain day before school started.

Northway, Alaska, had no reason to exist except for World War II. It was nothing more than an airport; still is. It had a gigantic hangar and a long fine runway. Flying the Alaska Highway meant a stop at White-horse—where they had knocked the top off a mountain to build an airport, so you walked down the mountain to get to town—and the next "hop" was three hundred miles away at Northway. From there, home.

I was a tired, cranky and butt-sore teenager. Northway was the last stop before Fairbanks. Land, gas up and take off; home before dark. We gobbled sandwiches in the coffee shop. I watched the guy gas the plane, always a good idea because they would sometimes "get it wrong"— always in their favor, of course. I briefly noticed a girl—her name was Cynthia—who was my age. She was the one waitress. She seemed to walk like the Pink Panther drawing attention to herself, seemed oddly top-heavy, and flirted with every man in the place. But not me.

I went with Mom to the flight office in the so-called terminal and heard the weather guy say no weather between Northway and Fairbanks; Mom filed the required flight plan. It was hot, clear, not a cloud visible. Actually, it seemed a little too hot. We took off. I settled back in my seat and began daydreaming about making the junior varsity basketball team—I had been "cut" as a freshman, but now I was a junior, bigger, stronger—and I had scored 12 points per game during the year I was enrolled as a sophomore at a funny-named school in Nashville, Peabody Demonstration School.

I had pulled my cap down low, trying to doze. Suddenly, Mom nudged me and pointed straight ahead. I had trouble understanding what I saw. It was a dark roiling cloud, almost black, stretching from above our altitude all the way to the ground. "Line squall," Mom muttered in a clipped unhappy voice. The term means a storm that has blown up out of nowhere. You go over it or around it. But if you're not sure how long it is, going around is not a good idea. This one stretched into the horizon. What had gone wrong? Don't we have the best Weather Service in the world?

We pressed on. Suddenly, Mom made a 180-degree turn. We were now heading back to another World War II artifact. It was the abandoned military airfield at Tanacross. Just land there, tie the plane down and wait for the weather to blow over.

We dropped to five hundred feet. Tarpaper was blowing off the old hangars there, flying across the runway. We headed back to Northway. When we landed at Northway, the weather was fine, just like it had been when we took off. We told the gas guy about the line squall. In Alaska, there is an expression for the look he gave Mom, a "shit-eating grin." I recognized it through the years. It's how men act to a woman they don't think knows what she is doing. He said nothing.

We asked the gas guy to help us push the plane into the hangar. Instead, he walked off. Mom got the tow bar and pulled on the nose wheel. I pushed on a wing strut. The plane got stuck on a railroad-like rail that the huge heavy doors rolled on. We struggled. Mom told me to push down on the tail. This lifted the front nose wheel enough to get it over the rail. We pushed the plane as far back into the hangar as we could.

I trailed a half step behind Mom. She went straight to the weather guy and told what happened. He looked at her blankly. He said nothing. She told everybody on the flight line about the line squall. The other pilots simply ignored her, got in their planes and took off.

Mom went to the office of the roadhouse (where the coffee shop was located) and insisted upon a room for the night, maybe two days, just in case. She went straight to the room and fell asleep. I loitered in the coffee shop. Nothing to do.

Thirty minutes later, the wind started blowing. Every plane that had taken off now returned. The pilots had serious looks on their faces. They demanded to put their planes in the hangar. The gas guy balked. Other planes seemed to come out of nowhere—anybody on his way from Whitehorse—anybody in the air within two hundred miles now made a detour to Northway. It looked like a picture from a movie, with planes making hurry-up landings on an aircraft carrier.

Then things got bad. Pilots who had tied down their planes now demanded to put their planes in the hangar. The gas guy's mouth was wide open. It looked like a fistfight was going to start, but the gas guy simply walked off.

It is strictly against flight (ground) rules to taxi an airplane into a hangar. You might lose control and crash into other parked planes. Start a fire causing millions in damage. But that is what happened; at least ten planes with propellers turning made it over that rail into the safety of the hangar.

A DC-3, a two-engine cargo plane used by the thousands in World War II, came in from Whitehorse. He gassed up took off for Fairbanks. Men always take chances, Mom had explained. Especially when they have a sturdy plane like a DC-3.

Any discussion of the relative merits of women pilots versus men pilots always gets around to Amelia Earhart. My whole life people had compared my mom to Amelia Earhart. If Mom was present, she nodded graciously, and said nothing except she had once met the famous lady pilot who was eleven years her senior.

Alone, the truth came out. "She was a lousy pilot. She got lost! Any woman could do what she did. She had what we didn't have, a millionaire husband. He bought her every plane she ever had, including two or three that she cracked up. She specialized in ground loops. (That's flight slang for crashing on takeoff.) Her husband was a famous publisher and he arranged massive publicity for her every flight."

Mom rarely said anything bad about anybody, but Amelia Earhart? She continued, "Her major contribution to women's flying was she popularized the wearing of slacks, but you can just as easily fly a plane in a skirt," Mom said. "You see, the real reason she wore slacks was because she had fat ankles, the slacks covered them up. Besides, she was good-looking. I wasn't."

While Mom dozed, the DC-3 had made two attempts to land. But the wind across the runway was fierce. As the plane neared the ground it was pushed almost sideways, making a landing too dangerous. On the third attempt, the pilot gave up and headed back to Whitehorse. At some level, I was disappointed. I've never seen a plane crash. And nobody pays enough attention to my mom, about nothing.

That evening a freak snowstorm pelted the airport. The wind howled. We slept snugly in our bunks. The entire coffee shop was filled with guys sleeping in chairs. Cynthia didn't show up the next morning so everybody poured his own coffee. The snow melted as quickly as it came. Normal weather returned.

Later that afternoon, we both struggled to help push the accumulated airplanes out of the hangar. Nobody said thanks. Nobody said anything. The Cessna 150 in the back looked small, but grateful. We pushed her over the rail, easier this time, and took off for Fairbanks.

When we arrived in Fairbanks, Mom and I took a cab straight to the superintendent of schools' office. We were too late and we knew it. But the lady at the desk took one of those rubber stamp machines that goes "ker-chunk" and stamped my mom's paper work. She said she'd give it to the superintendent in a flat voice that wasn't encouraging.

I looked at the paper work. So did Mom. We walked briskly out of the office. In the hall, Mom made a "ker-chunk" stamping motion and we both grinned. The lady had been too busy that morning to change the date on the stamp—it was two days behind the calendar. Mom got her raise; I made the basketball team, even played some on the varsity.

At Peabody Demonstration School we had spent what I thought was too much time simply learning vocabulary with flash cards. It was necessary for college entrance exams, they solemnly explained. But it seemed like cheating to me. One word I learned was "hubris," which means to have excessive pride or self-confidence.

I think of the word every time I think about Northway, or flying in Alaska. Here's why. Forgotten to history is the "Valley of the Three Million." It seems that six bombers were being ferried to Alaska. But there was only one navigator; the other planes simply followed by watching the lead plane. Actually, he was lost. The planes all plowed into mountains, killing everyone and destroying three million dollars worth of planes.

"Why couldn't they have used WASP pilots as navigators?" I asked Mom. She never said anything. She just went her way.

"I want to paddle my own canoe," was her motto. When she turned eighty she learned to fly ultra light aircraft. The FAA took away her flight certificate when she was only ninety-five, something about one of her eyes.

"But Wiley Post had only one eye, he even wore an eye patch!" she exclaimed.

"Mom," I replied, "he crashed at Barrow, just like Amelia Earhart, right?"

A Landing at Kokomo
by
Lewis L. Laska

Draw a line on a map from southern West Virginia to Fairbanks, Alaska. Avoid Chicago, always avoid Chicago. Veer west and then head north so that you land in Miles City, Montana. Mom had a woman pilot friend there, Vivienne. They had flown in the Powder Puff Derby, officially known as the All Women's Transcontinental Air-Race.

The Cessna 150 held only two people. Mom in the left seat was the pilot, I acted as co-pilot, kinda. This was sometime in the 1960s, I was a teenager. I knew most everything, of course, including quite a bit about flying. Mom had gotten her flight certificate in 1933, and had been a bush pilot in Alaska. That's where we were going, back to Fairbanks after a summer in the Lower 48. Another great summer at Camp Greenbrier in Alderson, West Virginia.

The plane was supposed to go one hundred miles an hour. It had an effective range of about three hundred miles; that meant three hours of butt time and everybody is ready to land. Mom had handed me the air chart to fold up and indicated we would land at Kokomo, Indiana.

It was a bright, beautiful late August day. The landing strip at Kokomo was perfectly inviting. True, it was a grass strip, not paved. There was no tower, hardly any planes on the ground. Just a windsock. Land, eat a cheeseburger, gas up and go. It was the first hop on a four thousand mile flight.

A perfect landing is one that is made in the first fifty feet of the strip. But this was not a perfect landing, just a near perfect one, perhaps a hundred feet down the five hundred foot strip. The tricycle landing gear entered the grass nicely. It always did; Mom never bounced on landing, never.

Nothing happened. The plane would not slow down. One of those mid-west rain showers had come through and the grass was soaking wet. But you could not see this from the air. The throttle ("the gas") was a knob on the dash. Push in to full throttle, pull out to shut off power.

The plane skittered atop the wet grass. Boys at Camp Greenbrier in West Virginia had known of this phenomenon. We had pretended to be baseball players sliding on butts and bellies through wet grass until we wore the grass down and it gave up on us. But not here.

The plane would not slow down. Yes, planes have brakes. The early ones, like the bi-plane my Mom learned to fly in, a Kinner Fleet, did not have brakes.

Mom pumped the brakes. It's an odd maneuver. The foot pedals actually control the rudder, used in making turns. But to brake, now that the plane is on the ground, the pilot presses her feet on the very top of the pedals. That activates the brakes. I could feel Mom feathering the brakes, off and on, kind of a tiptoe action. Almost funny. The actual weight of the plane needs to sink into the grass, not continue atop it.

How strange to sit in a plane with the prop stopped and the plane keeps going, like God is pushing it. No, we never gave the plane a name and did not refer to her as "she."

The end of the runway came rushing toward us. When it ended, there was still more grass, maybe fifty feet, but higher. Then a chain-link fence. Clearly, the fence would stop the plane, but at what damage? Would the prop get hung in the fence? Or flail away? Would we crack a wing? Would our faces hit the dashboard? Sure, we had seatbelts on, but so what?

The Cessna rushed onward. Mom stayed on her. The throttle ("gas") was long turned off, sticking out at us dumbly.

Suddenly, the plane gave a shudder. And another. She stopped abruptly. The chain link fence was fifteen feet away. Not much to do. Start the engine, taxi around.

Nothing to talk about—never did talk about it. Never. Gassed up again and we were gone.

Anybody can get a plane into the air. They practically jump into the air, especially light single-engine planes. The trick is a good landing.

"My Mom could land a plane on the back of a pick-up truck!" I told my class the day after her death at age 103 in 2012. They could not understand why a sixty-some year-old man would start crying.

"When everything seems to be going against you, remember that the airplane takes off against the wind, not with it."

—*Henry Ford*

AUTHOR'S NOTES

With all of these outstanding, talented women in their lives, it's easy for me to understand why those Bragg girls have "Braggin' Rights." Libby Coffin and Sandy Newell often refer to Homer Hickman's book, *We Are Not Afraid,* when they present their program "Braggin' Rights" to the public because he uses the following statements, which they feel adequately express the characteristics of their family.

We are proud of who we are.
We keep our families together.
We stand up for what we believe.
We trust in God but rely on ourselves.

***

Before completing this manuscript and sending it to my editors, I had the opportunity to take a flying lesson at Skywalker Flying in Adrian, Michigan. The owner, Jo Walker, is a seasoned pilot and introduced me to Steve Schankin, Certified Flight Instructor, who gave me my first lesson. He propped a couple pillows in my seat and walked me through the preflight checklist before he fired up the engine. While in the sky, I asked him various questions to help me understand some of the terminology and experiences that pilots such as Pearl must take into consideration while flying. For example, I immediately realized that I did not know where we were within five minutes after takeoff.

"I think I would get lost up here," I confessed.

"Yeah, pilots do from time to time," he replied.

"Really?"

"Uh-hum."

"It feels like we're floating. Are we going very fast?"

"Oh, about one hundred fifty miles per hour," he said.

"Wow. It doesn't feel like it."

"I know," he agreed, "it's pretty amazing isn't it?"

"Yes. It truly is."

"Are we going to ace a perfect landing?"

"We're going to try. But, either way tell Jo the landing was perfect."

"I will," I promised.

"Dee," he asked, "do you know the difference between a good landing and a perfect landing?"

I shrugged my shoulders. "No, what's the difference?"

"A good landing is one from which you can walk away. A perfect landing is one after which you can use the airplane another time."

I laughed. "Let's shoot for the perfect landing but I'll settle for a good one."

WASP Final Flight
Published by Wings Across America
Lelia Pearl Bragg Laska Chamberlain, 44-W-1T

November 22, 2012

Born Lelia Pearl Bragg on April 29, 1909, on Chestnut Mountain, Summers County, West Virginia, the former Fairbanks, Alaska, resident took her last flight on Thanksgiving Day, November 22, 2012, in Nashville, Tennessee. She was survived by her son, Nashville lawyer and college professor Lewis L. Laska. She was the last survivor of the nine children born at home to John W. and Lanie C. Bragg. She was a pioneer aviatrix and educator.

Pearl learned to fly in a Kinner Fleet Biplane in 1933 and held a pilot's certificate until she was 97. Prior to World War II, the federal government established the Civilian Flight Training Program, a back-door method to train pilots for military service. Because of its name, it had to allow participation of women and black men, both generally thought incapable of learning to fly in that era. Pearl was given the black students to instruct and each one she taught received his wings.

Pearl's regular occupation was as a public school teacher from the age of 17 until her retirement in 1972. She was a WASP (Women Air Force Service Pilot) trainee during the war and was honorably discharged. She also served as a cryptologist at the Pentagon where she received the first message from Guadalcanal.

In 1945, following her dream to be a full-time pilot, Pearl moved to Nome, Alaska, and worked as a flight instructor and bush pilot. The next year she became the first woman to solo a single-engine airplane (a 1939 Piper J4) up the Alaska Highway. The FAA recognized her achievements as a pioneer Alaskan aviator in 2006. Scorning the beliefs that Alaska Natives (Eskimos, etc.) were unable to learn flying, she taught many, including Holger Jorgensen, who became the first Native hired as a pilot by a scheduled airline.

In 1946, Pearl married Lewis Lincoln Laska, a merchant and fur dealer in McGrath, Alaska. Their son was born the next year. Lew, from a pioneer family, died four months later at the age of 50. Pearl continued to operate her husband's store and parka factory for another four years. She returned to teaching in Homer and then Fairbanks, Alaska. She continued to teach flying on the side. Her ground-based hobby was sewing fur parkas, mukluks and dolls. After several decades of summer school work, Pearl received an undergraduate degree from the University of Alaska in 1955. She received a master's degree from Miami University of Ohio in 1959 and her thesis was a history of civilian aviation in Alaska. A sabbatical leave spent at George Peabody College (now a part of Vanderbilt University), Nashville, in 1963-64 qualified her as the first special education teacher in Fairbanks.

The proud owner of a 1947 model Cessna 140 (and, later a Cessna 150), she flew these planes to the Lower 48 on numerous occasions. She flew several times in the All Women's Transcontinental Air Race ("Powder Puff Derby"). In later life she married a fellow schoolteacher, Ed Chamberlain, and they lived in California until his death in 1987. Thereafter, she drove her pickup to Fairbanks where she lived on her own, until she came to Nashville in 2006 to live with her son.

Gracious and even-tempered, Pearl allowed no nonsense when it came to flying, but asserted that every hour spent in the air gave a person an extra day on earth.

A life member of the 99's (The Association of Women Pilots), she did not follow the cult of Amelia Earhart (eleven years her senior) whom she met but did not know personally. "She got lost," was Pearl's final assessment of "AE" whom she recognized as an important pathfinder in women's aviation. The wearing of slacks was Amelia's greatest contribution to women, insisted Pearl, who said it was just as easy to fly in a skirt as well. Pearl insisted that Jacqueline Cochran, a few years older than she, and Jerri Cobb, much younger, were the best women pilots of the era.

Oma Bragg O'Bryan's poems are used by permission of her daughters, Libby O'Bryan Coffin and Sandy O'Bryan Newell.

Biographical Sketch Oma Bragg O'Bryan
Published in *Sunrise Beyond*

The writer at the time of sending these poems to the publisher was just recovering from major eye surgery on both eyes—one operation in June 1983 and the second in July 1984. This darkness undoubtedly had some influence upon her subjects and expressions. However, in rare writings of the time this did not show up—somehow the world of darkness—unlike Milton when he wrote, "On His Blindness," was a subject not easily touched upon.

Oma did enjoy being called upon to give a book review of *The Life of Emily Dickinson* at one writers' group of a Senior Center in Florida. For the next meeting the group asked her to give a review of her own book. They entitled the program—Emily Dickinson Returns.

Oma Bragg O'Bryan
June 18, 1913 – June 11, 2003

Oma Bragg O'Bryan, 89, died Wednesday, June 11, 2003. A memorial service was held in the one-room school on Chestnut Mountain. She lived a long life as a mother, wife, teacher, poet and artist.

She was born June 18, 1913, in Hinton. She graduated from Sandstone High School in West Virginia, where she walked down the mountain to school and home again while studying birds and fleeing wildcats. She received a bachelor's degree from Concord College and started her teaching career in the one-room schools of Summers County, West Virginia.

In 1953, she and her family moved to Fort White, were she taught second grade. After moving to Lake City, Oma introduced families to the creative world of art through the Columbia County Adult Education program.

Today, Sandy Newell and Elizabeth Coffin, her daughters, carry on this legacy of learning with careers in public libraries, public education and encouraging others to learn about their own family history.

References and Notes

Cover Photo by Bessewisser99 (Own work) CC BY-SA 3.0 via Wikimedia Commons (https://creativecommons.org/licenses/by-sa/3.0).

Chamberlain, Pearl Bragg Laska. "From My Logbook." *Western Flyer*. October 1980.

Coffin, Elizabeth O'Bryan. & Newell, Sandra O'Bryan. Script from the program *Braggin' Rights*. 2011.

Faulconer, J.E. "Pearl of the North from Summers." *Hinton Daily News*. May 14, 1976.

Gwinn, Adrian. "Hillbilly 'Eskimo'." *Charleston Daily Mail*. May 4, 1976.

Hickman, Homer. "We Are Not Afraid." Florida: Health Communications, Inc. February 1, 2002.

Laska, Lewis, L. "Letter to Pearl Laska." Personal Correspondence. April 24, 2003.

Laska, Lewis, L., *A Landing at Kokomo*, and *A Take-Off at Northway*.

National Women's History Project and Carol Gold, UAF History and Women's Studies. "Above it All: A History of Women's History Month." *Heartland Magazine*. March 8, 1998.

Newell, Sandra O'Bryan. "The Chestnut Mountain Home," 1969 and 2001.

O'Bryan, Oma Bragg. "Where I Long To Go." New York: Vantage Press. 1985.

O'Bryan, Oma Bragg. "Sunrise Beyond." West Virginia: McClain Printing Company. 1985.

Roth, Pauline Bragg. "She Was One Of Them—I Wasn't." *The Senior Tribune.* December 1984.

Smith, Barbara B. "Her Place in the Sky." *Heartland Magazine.* March 8, 1998.

Sumner, Sandi. "Women Pilots of Alaska." North Carolina: McFarland and Company. January 6, 2005.

The Gregg-Laska Store. Information compiled with the help of Pearl Bragg Laska Chamberlain, Florence and Oscar Winchell and Pat Wachel. April 18, 1986.

Portions of this novel are taken from Pearl Bragg Laska Chamberlain's unpublished short stories and include renditions of the follow tales:

To Grandpa Cales
Old Scratchers
A Sad Day
Pandora's Box
Candy or Cheese
An Early Menopause
The Fallen Leaf
School Days
Aladdin's Lamp
Soft Soap and Hard Work
Willard
Mr. Copeland's School
Mandy's God
Untitled Story
The Empty Pocketbook
The Possum Ridge Turn Around
The Blue Flame
Bet Dies
Pi (3.1416) in the Sky
Alaska
Peter's Bath
Jonathan and David
Mobile Home to Alaska/The Long Haul

Margaret Van Cleve interviewed Pearl Laska Chamberlain on May 24, 1991, at the sound studio at Elmer E. Rasmuson Library at the University of Alaska Fairbanks in Fairbanks, Alaska. In this interview, Pearl talks about learning to fly in a man's world, the struggles with getting work as a pilot, flying to Alaska, and her love of flying. If you would like to hear the interview, the link is attached:

https://jukebox.uaf.edu/site7/interviews/2527

Project Jukebox
Digital Branch of the University of Alaska Fairbanks Oral History Program

Pearl's granddaughter, Jennava L. Laska, wrote the following blog and has included some wonderful photographs of Pearl. Jennava is an accomplished filmmaker and furniture designer. She has two degrees in film production from Art Center College of Design in Pasadena.

http://pearllaskachamberlain.blogspot.com

Newspaper article about 1958 Powder Puff Derby entitled, "Powder Puff Air Race is Complete"

https://news.google.com/newspapers?nid=1928&dat=19580709&id=iEc pAAAAIBAJ&sjid=MWgFAAAAIBAJ&pg=902,707001&hl=en

Pearl graduated from high school in Hinton, West Virginia, which was not far from her home on Chestnut Mountain.

http://www.hintonwva.com/about

Jackson's Mill State 4-H Camp Historic District, also known as West Virginia University Jackson's Mill, is a historic 4-H camp and national historic district near Weston, Lewis County, West Virginia. The Bragg family visited the camp often and this is where Pearl first decided she wanted to learn to fly.

https://jacksonsmill.wvu.edu/heritage-education

Pearl experienced many great adventures while living in Nome, Alaska, which are mentioned in this novel. She spent a great deal of time working as a bush pilot while living here.
http://www.visitnomealaska.com

In 1945, Pearl moved to McGrath, Alaska, where she met and married the love of her life, Lew Laska. Pearl spent many years in this lovely town, running her late husband's store and working as a bush pilot.
http://mtnt.net/mcgrath.php

After leaving McGrath, Pearl and her son, Lewis, moved to Fairbanks, Alaska, where she lived for many years. The mayor of Fairbanks actually declared a "Pearl Laska Chamberlain Day" in her honor.
https://www.explorefairbanks.com

(Pearl with her son Lewis)

(Sandy Newell and Libby Coffin)

<

Libby, Kate, who is Libby's granddaughter, Pearl and Lewis

Grandpa and Grandma Cales

>

<

John and Laney Bragg
65th Anniversary

Thank you for taking the time to read
Pearl: You are Cleared to Land.
I hope you enjoyed it!

Made in the USA
Columbia, SC
04 May 2018